The Open Secret of Ireland

CLASSICS OF IRISH HISTORY
General Editor: Tom Garvin

Original publication dates of reprinted titles are given in brackets

P. S. O'Hegarty, *The Victory of Sinn Féin* (1924)
Walter McDonald, *Some Ethical Questions of Peace and War* (1919)
Joseph Johnston, *Civil War in Ulster* (1913)
James Mullin, *The Story of a Toiler's Life* (1921)
Robert Brennan, *Ireland Standing Firm* and *Eamon de Valera* (1958)
Mossie Harnett, *Victory and Woe: The West Limerick Brigade
in the War of Independence*
Padraig de Burca and John F. Boyle, *Free State or Republic?
Pen Pictures of the Historic Treaty Session of Dáil Éireann* (1922)
Arthur Clery, *The Idea of a Nation* (1907)
Standish James O'Grady, *To the Leaders of Our Working People*
Michael Davitt, *Jottings in Solitary*
Oliver MacDonagh, *Ireland: The Union and its Aftermath* (1977)
Thomas Fennell, *The Royal Irish Constabulary: A History and Personal Memoir*
Arthur Griffith, *The Resurrection of Hungary* (1918)
William McComb, *The Repealer Repulsed* (1841)
George Moore, *Parnell and His Island* (1887)
Charlotte Elizabeth Tonna, *Irish Recollections* (1841/47 as *Personal Recollections*)
Standish James O'Grady, *Sun and Wind*
John Sarsfield Casey, *The Galtee Boy: A Fenian Prison Narrative*
William and Mary Ann Hanbidge, *Memories of West Wicklow: 1813–1939* (1939)
A. P. A. O'Gara, *The Green Republic* (1902)
William Cooke Taylor, *Reminiscences of Daniel O'Connell* (1847)
William Bruce and Henry Joy, *Belfast Politics* (1794)
Annie O'Donnell, *Your Fondest Annie*
Joseph Keating, *My Struggle for Life* (1916)
John Mitchel, *The Last Conquest of Ireland (Perhaps)* (1858/9)
Harold Begbie, *The Lady Next Door* (1914)
Eugene Davis, *Souvenirs of Footprints Over Europe* (1889)
Maria Edgeworth, *An Essay on Irish Bulls* (1802)
D. P. Moran, *The Philosophy of Irish Ireland* (1898–1900)
Thomas Kettle, *The Open Secret of Ireland* (1912)

The Open Secret of Ireland

⁛

THOMAS KETTLE

With an introduction by
J. E. Redmond, M.P.

edited by Senia Pašeta

UNIVERSITY COLLEGE DUBLIN PRESS
Preas Choláiste Ollscoile Bhaile Átha Cliath

First published by W. J. Ham-Smith, London, 1912
This edition first published by
University College Dublin Press, 2007
Introduction to this edition © Senia Pašeta 2007

ISBN 978-1-904558-76-7
ISSN 1393-6883

University College Dublin Press
Newman House, 86 St Stephen's Green
Dublin 2, Ireland
www.ucdpress.ie

Cataloguing in Publication data available
from the British Library

Typeset in France in Ehrhardt by Elaine Burberry
Text design by Lyn Davies, Frome, Somerset, England
Printed in England on acid-free paper by Athenæum Press Ltd

CONTENTS

Note on the Text

The text has been re-set from the 1912 edition published in London by W. J. Ham-Smith.

INTRODUCTION
Senia Pašeta

Thomas Michael Kettle, known for most of his life as Tom, was born at Artane, County Dublin on 9 February 1880. He was the seventh of the twelve children of the farmer and rural activist, Andrew Kettle and his wife Margaret McCourt. The Kettle family was brought up in relative comfort as Andrew Kettle made a good living from growing barley and breeding cattle and horses. Most of the children were born in Millview, a 'long, rambling, two-storey house' in Malahide, though the family moved several times as it expanded. Margaret Kettle appears to have been well loved by her children, possibly because their father was rather more stern and demanding than his much younger wife. Kettle senior was a strict disciplinarian who did not suffer fools gladly and this appeared to have resulted in a less than cosy family life.

The Kettle children grew up surrounded by political activity and intrigue. Andrew Kettle boasted an impressive nationalist pedigree, having been a member of the Tenant League in the 1850s and becoming a confidant of Charles Stewart Parnell. He had presided at the first meeting of the Land League in 1870, and had signed the 'No Rent Manifesto' before serving a prison sentence for his involvement in land agitation in 1881. He attempted to avoid exposing his children to politics, but it is clear that at least his son Thomas became interested at an early age. He also inherited his father's love of literature and his devotion to the Catholic faith.

The Kettle brothers were very well educated by the standards of the day, a reflection of their family's social standing and means. They were sent initially to the Christian Brothers before Thomas and Lawrence (Larry) Kettle were dispatched in 1894 to Andrew Kettle's own *alma mater*, Clongowes Wood College, Ireland's most prestigious Catholic school. Thomas Kettle was exposed at the Jesuit-run boarding school to some of the social and intellectual pursuits which were to influence profoundly his subsequent political activity. He embraced sports at Clongowes, excelling at cricket and establishing with his brother a cycling club. His intellectual prowess became apparent soon after he began at Clongowes, but his wife subsequently claimed that he did not enjoy Clongowes, feeling himself to be stifled by an intermediate education system which reduced learning to a memory work and competitive examinations. He displayed his intellectual individuality by electing to take German rather than Greek as was usual, and by reading well beyond what was expected by the examiners. Despite his reservations, he excelled academically, taking prizes for English and French compositions and a gold medal for first place in English in his final examinations.

The obvious next step was the Jesuit-administered University College Dublin (UCD), successor to Newman's old Catholic University and the most prestigious of all Catholic university colleges then affiliated with the Royal University of Ireland. Kettle went to UCD in 1897, joining a remarkable group of young men, many of whom were to achieve prominence in twentieth-century Ireland and at least one, James Joyce, who became world famous. UCD at the turn of the twentieth century was, according to Arthur Clery (fellow student and future professor of law at UCD), 'undescribaly [*sic*] brilliant and interesting"[1] and Kettle found himself at the heart of its vibrant political and intellectual activity.[2]

It was through the college's Literary and Historical Society (the 'L&H') that most topical issues were debated and it quickly became known as a training ground for Ireland's future political elite. Kettle became auditor of the L&H for the 1898–9 session, but he was forced to resign in 1900 and he also failed to sit his university examinations that year. The ill-health which interrupted his university career was likely to have been some form of nervous breakdown, a condition which was to haunt him periodically in the future. His health broke down again in 1903, due, according to his wife, to 'shattered nerves' and the death of his beloved brother, William.[3] His solace during such traumatic times was often continental travel, a pursuit which allowed him to improve his French and his German, and to develop his ideas about Ireland's relationship with Europe. His subsequent insistence that 'in order to become deeply Irish, [Ireland] must become European',[4] owed much to his trips abroad and his love of the continent would inform some of his dearest held positions.

Kettle finally took his degree in 1902 and entered the Honourable Society of King's Inns as a law student in the following year. By the time he was called to the Bar in 1906, he had served as auditor of the Literary Society and had won both the Gold Medal for Oratory and the Victoria Prize. But, unlike several of his UCD contemporaries, he did not pursue a legal career with any real enthusiasm, turning instead to journalism and politics. Kettle's deep and enduring attachment to UCD proved invaluable in this endeavour. In 1903, he became editor of *St Stephen's*, a lively UCD newspaper, and he also began to contribute frequently to the *Freeman's Journal* and periodicals including the *New Ireland Review*. With friend and former fellow student, Francis Sheehy Skeffington, he founded and edited the short-lived but provocative *Nationist*, 'a weekly review of Irish thought and affairs'.

Kettle's keen interest in politics ensured that he kept a close eye on such new political organisations as Sinn Féin, but he remained to the core a constitutional nationalist: he welcomed new initiatives, but he urged gaelicists, constitutionalists and separatists alike to maintain nationalist unity behind the leadership of the Irish Parliamentary Party (IPP). In 1904 he demonstrated still further his dedication to the IPP by helping to found and becoming president of the Young Ireland Branch (YIB) of the United Irish League (UIL). The YIB was progressive in that it stated that no distinction of 'sex, class or creed' be placed on its membership. It was the only branch of the UIL which welcomed women and its constituency reflected a variety of nationalist opinion, ranging from moderate Home Rule to near separatism. Kettle's own brand of nationalism was located somewhere in the middle. He had flirted with some advanced nationalist ideas and he understood the appeal of the new cultural movements. He was more aware than most constitutional nationalists of their potential to capture the loyalty of younger nationalists, and he urged the Party leadership to show more interest in cultural nationalism in particular. But he remained resolute in his conviction that all nationalists must ultimately submit to the leadership and the direction of the Irish Party as it offered the best chance of securing home rule. Such a position became more and more untenable as the early optimism surrounding the third Home Rule Bill gave way to bitterness and disappointment. As Shane Leslie put it:

> He seemed destined to fulfil a vital but never quite attainable part in Irish life, to reconcile the old generation of Parliamentarians with the new Ireland which had arisen to demand better things . . . his friends were the young Irelanders who were already breaking in sympathy with the Irish party. He alone could have wrought a reconciliation and possibly averted the terrible revolt which buried so much promise in the

ruins of Dublin. He was early aware of the restiveness of young men and of the necessity of supplying them with a place in the National movement before they chose one for themselves.[5]

The party leader, John Redmond, had identified Kettle's potential and had urged him to stand for parliament in 1904. Kettle declined on that occasion but agreed in 1906 to contest a by-election for the seat of East Tyrone. Kettle won the seat by the narrow margin of 18 votes, becoming one of the very few young men to be accepted into the ageing ranks of the Party in the early years of the twentieth century. He maintained his links with the YIB while an MP, though he found himself on more than one occasion defending the Party against the criticism of some of his former student colleagues, a number of whom would, like most of nationalist Ireland, subsequently break with the Party while Kettle continued to defend it.

Kettle looked set to enjoy a glittering parliamentary career: Balfour declared that Kettle's was the best maiden speech he had ever heard and his reputation as a gifted orator and fine essayist grew. In 1909 he married his long-term sweetheart, Mary Sheehy, a well-known suffragette and fellow YIB. She too boasted impeccable nationalist credentials: her father was an Irish Party MP and her Uncle Eugene was known as the 'the Land League Priest'. In the following year he retained the loyalty of his constituents, re-contesting and winning his Tyrone seat in early 1910 with an increased majority, beating the well-known son of Colonel Saunderson. Yet, only months later, he informed his constituents in mid-1910 that he would not stand at the next election unless the party could provide him with an uncontested seat.[6]

He nevertheless retained a staunch loyalty to the IPP, despite the battering it was to take over its failure to force Asquith's Liberals to face down Ulster resistance to the 1912 Home Rule Bill. It was thus almost inevitable that he was to join, after some initial reluctance, the Volunteers, and was determined to guard against a separatist takeover of the organisation and, as he saw it, to defend the Home Rule Bill. He was sent in mid-1914 to Belgium to buy guns for the Volunteers, but his mission coincided with the German invasion of the country, shifting his political priorities fundamentally. Having witnessed the brutality of the German forces, Kettle declared 'it is impossible not to be with Belgium in the struggle. It is impossible any longer to be passive'.[7]

Kettle became a war correspondent before throwing himself into recruiting and propaganda work for the allied cause. This inevitably earned him the wrath of advanced nationalists, and thus exposed him to ridicule and strain which, given his poor mental and physical health, he found hard to bear. Probably most wounding were the accusations that while he urged young men to fight, he hid behind a recruiter's uniform. Kettle had in fact attempted to secure an active commission on many occasions, initially on his return from Belgium. Having been given the rank of Lieutenant and assigned to recruitment duties instead, he made a number of subsequent applications; they were all rejected because of his 'ill health', an oblique reference to his alcoholism which he had been unable to overcome, despite treatment.

The years leading up to his death in 1916 were in many ways the most wretched of his life: humiliated by the jeers of the underground press, unable to curb his drinking, and his candidature for an East Galway by-election in 1914 rejected, he was a man whose early promise seemed to have come to little. He was finally given permission in 1916 to be sent on active duty with the 16th Irish Division's 9th Royal Dublin Fusiliers. He welcomed the chance to redeem his reputation and having apparently weaned himself off alcohol, he left Ireland for the last time on 14 July. Kettle's belief that Ireland had a moral duty to stand up to German aggression did not waver during his last months. He was certainly critical at times of the commercialisation of the war and of the War Office itself, but he also maintained that common participation in the war effort could harmonise and strengthen relations between nationalists and unionists and between Britain and Ireland. Such sentiments appear exceptionally simplistic, especially in the aftermath of the Easter Rising, but he was by no means unique in holding them and they were no less deeply held for their naivety.

Kettle was killed on 9 September 1916, as he led his Division's 'B' company out of its trench during the attack on Ginchy. He died immediately having been shot in the heart. Shortly before he died, he had written to a friend: 'I am myself quite extraordinarily happy. If it should come my way to die I shall sleep well in the France I always loved, and shall know that I have done something towards bringing to birth the Ireland one has dreamed of'.[8] As a committed Home Ruler, critic of the excesses of the Gaelic League and a champion of Irish war participation, his reputation was bound to suffer in post-revolutionary Ireland. His recent rehabilitation owes much to the activists and scholars who have doggedly worked to recover Ireland's Great War dead, as well his own passionate and now appealing Europeanism. He was, in the words of Shane Leslie, 'an international Nationalist, which is as rare in Ireland as elsewhere'.[9] This deeply held and brilliantly articulated outlook has made Kettle an immensely attractive symbol for modern Ireland and has suggested the existence of alternative worlds of ideas and aspirations in an Ireland whose political future was anything but predestined.

THE OPEN SECRET OF IRELAND

The Open Secret of Ireland was written against the backdrop of mounting debate and rumour about the third Home Rule Bill. Speculation about a potential bill had been rife since late 1909, when Prime Minister Asquith stated that the Liberal Party would recommence its Home Rule campaign, delighting most constitutional nationalists and acknowledging the Irish Party's probable crucial role in the Liberals' electoral strategy. By the spring of 1910, the country found itself in the middle of a constitutional crisis, a crisis which promised almost certain rewards for the Irish Party. Expectations were exceptionally high in nationalist Ireland.

Kettle's *Open Secret of Ireland* should be viewed both within the context of this unfolding debate and as a product of an exceptionally jubilant and confident nationalism. It was written at the peak of the Irish Party's success, before the Home Rule debate became the Home Rule 'crisis'. In late 1911, when Kettle finished his book he, like most constitutional nationalists, believed that the parliamentary future of the Home Rule Bill was 'safe',[10] and this helps to explain the tone of his book.

The Open Secret was different from most of Kettle's publications in that its target audience was chiefly British. It aimed, according to the introduction by John Redmond, to enable 'Englishmen to view the Anglo-Irish question from the standpoint of an educated and friendly Irish opinion'. Kettle was ideally placed to offer such a perspective, being well regarded as an intellectual, politician and writer. More importantly, he was not known for his animosity towards England or the English people, emphasising regularly instead many of the common political and cultural values of the two nations.[11]

As the Home Rule Bill became ever more embroiled in controversy, he was to reinforce this point more often, no doubt hoping to counter the charge that Home Rule represented merely the thin edge of the separatist wedge. Kettle's loyalty to Ireland was tempered by a respect for constitutional procedures and tradition and, like Redmond, he believed passionately in an important role for Ireland and Irish citizens in the British Empire.[12] He had been a fierce critic of the Boer War, but he also maintained that the Empire contained within itself the seeds of its own regeneration. Similarly, while he plainly stated that Britain had 'failed' in Ireland, he insisted that the potential for harmonious Anglo-Irish relations remained good – so long as Home Rule was conceded. He represented, in many ways, the acceptable face of Irish nationalism, and an appealing alternative both to unrestrained unionism and rabid separatism, and Redmond surely had this firmly in mind when he agreed to write the effusive introduction to the book.

The Open Secret of Ireland was one of a series of roughly contemporaneous publications on Home Rule, including Erskine Childers's *The Framework of Home Rule* and Stephen Gwynn's *Case for Home Rule* as well as Kettle's own *Home Rule Finance: An Experiment in Justice*, all published in 1911. The time was of course ripe for such publications as they all sought to mould public opinion in favour of the Home Rule Bill, and Kettle's own work nicely complemented this growing body of pro-Home Rule literature. But a comparison of *The Open Secret of Ireland* with some of these other publications reveals a great deal about Kettle's own strengths and weaknesses as a writer and indeed about some of the inherent difficulties in attempting to win over sceptical audiences. Kettle was, for example, notoriously short on detail about exactly how Ireland's political system would operate under Home Rule. This was no doubt partly due to the fact that the details of the constitutional status of Ireland under Home Rule had not yet been decided, let alone published, and Kettle must have been acutely aware of the inherent dangers in over speculation.

But his insistence on writing in general terms about the unfolding of democracy in post-Home Rule Ireland was also a reflection of his wider tendency to avoid detail in favour of flourish and big ideas. This is not to suggest that he had not the capacity to absorb detail: his mastery of several European languages and literary and philosophical fields suggest exactly the opposite, but his forte and his strengths were big ideas, the impressive integration of a wide variety of philosophical, political and economic theories and, more simply, his wit, his beautiful writing style and his sheer mastery of the English language. George O'Brien, one of Kettle's first tutees at UCD and a future professor of economics at the same institution, neatly captured this ability in his description of Kettle as 'a professor of things in general'.[13]

Unlike most Home Rule propagandists Kettle was a genuinely talented writer, and he put that to excellent use in a text whose purpose was to convince without presenting the kinds of unmoveable demands and master plans which could inflame opponents of the bill. *The Open Secret of Ireland* was thus a wide-ranging, genial but determined attempt to persuade English audiences that Home Rule was inevitable and that Ireland's 'open secret' was in fact its nationhood, a nationhood which warranted political autonomy. It was a message which was designed to appeal to a broad range of opinion in a voice which suggested that Anglo-Irish co-operation and friendship were not only possible, but necessary if both nations were to prosper.

Some of Kettle's wider preoccupations and prejudices also informed this book. It is interesting, for example, that never once was the necessity of the Irish language mentioned, let alone advocated, in many of the lengthy passages on nationhood. This was a reflection of his suspicion of prescriptive Gaelicism and also most likely yet another attempt to avoid discussion of what he considered to be some of the less rational – and less appealing and comprehensible to his English audience – manifestations of Irish nationalism. His presentation of himself and his fellow home rulers as modern, rational and reasonable was also emphasised in sections which dealt with the management of the Irish economy and resources under Home Rule. He once again avoided detail, arguing that his book's aim was not to precipitate the great debates which would accompany the construction and passage of the Home Rule Bill, but to explain some of the foundation of the 'Home Rule idea'. This was surely deliberate as Kettle must have been aware that the actual economic provisions of the Home Rule Bill were going to be the most difficult to formulate and to reach agreement on.

The economics of Irish nationalism became ever more important to Kettle as his formal political career petered out. He wrote the *Open Secret* only a year after giving up his East Tyrone seat, describing it at times, according to his biographer, as his 'Bettystown book' as it was largely written at Bettystown, County Louth, where the family spent their summer holidays.[14] The book was a clear indication that his devotion to constitutional Home Rule had not abated as a result. Why he pulled out of parliamentary politics after regaining his seat in 1910 remains a matter of some debate, especially as the passage of a successful Home Rule Bill through the parliament then looked more feasible than it had for generations. It is most likely he stood down from a combination of exhaustion, frustration and severe financial strain. In addition, he had accepted a Chair in National Economics in UCD in 1909. Arthur Clery claimed that Kettle hoped to be able to hold both his seat and the professorship, and counted on the party rejecting his resignation. After it was accepted, Clery claimed that Kettle's career was simply one 'of despair'.[15] Certainly, his acceptance of the UCD position had exposed him to charges of corruption and jobbery, and these had worn him down. Although he attempted to combine politics and academe for a time, by 1910 he admitted that he could not do justice to both. The £500 stipend attached to the professorship no doubt played a large part in his decision, as he had struggled on his small party stipend. But Kettle had also developed a serious alcohol problem by this time and it is difficult to see how he could have sustained such a demanding programme, especially as he continued to suffer bouts of depression.

Kettle was stung by the furore which had greeted his UCD appointment, not least because of the intellectual objections raised to the very notion of a chair in 'National' economics and Kettle's own suitability for any kind of academic position, let alone one in economics. These accusations were somewhat unfair as Kettle had long been a keen, though by no means expert, commentator on economic questions, especially as they applied to Ireland and he was deeply interested in political economy. As his friend J. J. Hogan argued, Kettle's intellectual interest in Irish politics led invariably to a serious consideration of Irish economic conditions. As a parliamentarian, he had been acknowledged as an authority on Irish economic matters; he had served on the Public Accounts Committee and he co-authored *Old Age Pensions Act 1908*, and produced *Home Rule Finance*.

Economic questions were thus clearly on Kettle's mind when he sat down to write *The Open Secret*. Its publication presented an opportunity to hit back at his critics and to justify his appointment. In addition, focusing on what he described as the economic exploitation of Ireland allowed him to showcase and contrast his considered, intellectual and studied economic ideas with those of some of the advanced nationalists like Griffith who, Kettle believed, relied too much on hyperbole and too little on fact. Kettle's critique of Ireland's economic exploitation is the focus of the two chapters on 'The Ravages of Unionism', financial matters probably being singled out because they allowed the kind of scientific analysis Kettle favoured. Kettle's approach to the issue was relatively unusual as it relied on a combination of philosophy, raw data and economic theory, but its conclusion that Ireland's economy had suffered through a variety of flawed policies including the Poor Laws, the Land Laws and over taxation under the Union settlement was a variety of a standard nationalist trope.

It is likely, however, that Kettle's economic critique was designed as much to counter dire unionist predictions about Ireland's economy under Home Rule as it was to appeal to the rational English reader. Kettle had never made much of an attempt to pander to unionist sensibilities, displaying instead the not untypical nationalist disdain for the creed ('largely a phenomenon of hysteria') and its rank and file. His position could not have been made plainer in his chapter on 'the hallucinations of "Ulster"', a sharp and unapologetic assessment of the unionist case against Home Rule. In contrast to his usually well-considered reflections on Irish politics, Kettle's position on Ulster was naïve and based on the central idea that Ulster was bluffing. This was hardly uncommon among nationalists, very few of whom attempted to evaluate Ulster's position in anything but the most dismissive way. Nationalists writing during this critical period were of course highly unlikely to produce sympathetic critiques of Irish unionism, but it is clear that Kettle's position in *The Open Secret* was a deeply and long-held one, and not merely a response to the current crisis.[16] For all its wit and humour, it was ultimately to be proved flawed and unhelpful.

Unionists beyond the 'unbridged waters of the Boyne' and the smoke-filled rooms of Westminster hardly figured in his considerations: unionism, for Kettle, appeared to have little purchase in southern Ireland. Nevertheless, Kettle identified 'the pivot' upon which Ulster Unionism resided as the Library of the Four Courts in Dublin, led of course by Edward Carson and his fellow King's Counsellors. The lack of agency with which he endowed the plain people of the north of Ireland was a clear expression of his misunderstanding of the depth of political feeling and commitment to be found among them. By 1916 he had a surer grasp of the tenacity of this political allegiance, but he nonetheless continued to hope until his last days that unionist and nationalist would find common cause through collective sacrifice in the bloody trenches of Belgium and France.

This was an aspiration whose infeasibility Kettle underestimated in a way which could almost be described as delusional, but it should also be seen as the aspiration of an ultimately defeated but nonetheless significant section of the nationalist community. *The Open Secret of Ireland* should be read with a view to understanding some of the ideas which were held by the constitutional nationalists of Kettle's era and persuasion – as one testament of their faith in the logic and eventuality of Home Rule, as written by one of the brightest exponents of its possibilities.

Notes to Introduction

1 A. E. Clery, *Dublin Essays* (Dublin, 1919), p. 55.

2 For UCD at this time see: Patrick Maume, *The Long Gestation: Nationalist Political Life, 1891–1918* (Dublin, 1999) and Senia Pašeta, *Before the Revolution: Nationalism, Social Change and Ireland's Catholic Elite, 1879–1922* (Cork, 1999).

3 Mary Kettle, 'Memoir', in T. M. Kettle, *The Ways of War* (London, 1917), p. 15.

4 T. M. Kettle, Introduction to *The Day's Burden: Studies, Literary and Political and Miscellaneous Essays* (London, 1917), pp. xi–xii.

5 Shane Leslie, *The Irish Issue in its American Aspect* (London, 1918), pp. 97–8.

6 *The Times*, 17 Nov. 1910.

7 *Daily News*, 8 Aug. 1914.

8 T. M. Kettle to H. McLaughlin, 7 Aug. 1916, T. M. Kettle Papers, LA34/397, UCD.

9 Leslie, *The Irish Issue*, p. 101.

10 See p. 7 below.

11 See, for example, Pašeta, *Before the Revolution*, p. 132.

12 Ibid., pp. 131–2.

13 J. Meenan, *George O'Brien: A Biographical Memoir* (Dublin, 1980), pp. 30–1.

14   J. B. Lyons, *The Enigma of Tom Kettle: Irish Patriot, Essayist, Poet, British Soldier, 1880–1916* (Dublin, 1983), p. 213.

15   Clery, *Dublin Essays*, p. 11.

16   See: Senia Pašeta, *Thomas Kettle*, Irish Historical Association, 2007 (forthcoming).

The Open Secret of Ireland

✦

Also it is a proverbe of olde date, 'The pride of Fraunce, the treason of Inglande, and the warre of Irelande, shall never have ende.' Which proverbe, touching the warre of Irelande, is like alwaie to continue, without God sette in men's breasts to find some new remedy that never was found before.

State Papers, Reign of Henry VIII

INTRODUCTION

The object of Mr Kettle, in writing this book, is, I take it, to reveal to English readers what he not inaptly terms as 'The Open Secret of Ireland', in order to bring about a better understanding between the two nations, and to smoothe the way to a just and final settlement of their old-time differences. Any work undertaken on such lines commends itself to a ready welcome and a careful study, and I feel sure that both await Mr Kettle's latest contribution to the literature of the Irish question. As the son of one of the founders of the Land League, and as, for some years, one of the most brilliant members of the Irish Party, and, later, Professor in the School of Economics in the new National University in Dublin, he has won his way to recognition as an eloquent exponent of Irish national ideas; whilst the novelty of his point of view, and the freshness, vigour, and picturesque attractiveness of his style ensure for his work a cordial reception on its literary merits, apart from its political value.

Undoubtedly, one of the main sources of the Anglo-Irish difficulty has been mutual misunderstanding, generating mutual mistrust and hatred. But the root of the difficulty goes deeper. It is to be sought in the system of misgovernment and oppression which successive generations of British rulers have imposed upon what, with cruel irony, British historians and statesmen have been wont to call 'the sister country'. This is the real 'open secret' of Ireland, a secret that all who run may read, and the effective bearing of which is: that tyranny begets hatred, and that freedom and justice are the only sure foundations of contentment and goodwill between nations.

During the past thirty years, and especially since 1886, when Mr Gladstone threw the weight of his unrivalled genius and influence into the scale in favour of justice to Ireland, a great deal has been done to erase the bitter memories of the past, and to enable the English and the Irish peoples to regard each other in the light of truth, and with a more just appreciation of what is essential to the establishment of genuine and lasting friendly relations between them.

But it would be idle to ignore the fact that, to a considerable section of the English people, Ireland is still a country of which they possess less knowledge than they do of the most insignificant and remote of the many islands over which the British flag floats. Mr Kettle's book ought to be of service in dispelling this ignorance, and in enabling Englishmen to view the Anglo-Irish question from the standpoint of an educated and friendly Irish opinion.

The output of purely political literature on the Irish problem has been increasing during the past few years, and there is room for a book which aims at focussing attention upon some aspects of it which the mere politician is apt to pass lightly over or to ignore altogether. Like most of Mr Kettle's work, the book bears the impress of his individuality, and, to many of his readers, this will constitute much of its charm and merit. At the same time, in order to prevent misunderstanding, it is necessary for me to state that I do not commit myself to acceptance or endorsement of everything which the book contains. I content myself with stating, from personal experience, that nothing which Mr Kettle writes about Ireland can fail to be worthy of notice by everyone interested in the Home

Rule controversy, and that I believe the circulation of this volume will serve to stimulate thought about Ireland, and so to hasten the advent of that brighter day when the grant of full self-government to Ireland will reveal to England the open secret of making Ireland her friend and helpmate, the brightest jewel in her crown of Empire.

J. E. REDMOND
12 December 1911

PRELIMINARY

After an intermission of nearly twenty years Ireland once again blocks the way. 'Finally rejected' by the House of Commons and the English electorate in 1886, 'finally rejected' by the House of Lords in 1893, the Home Rule idea has not only survived but waxed stronger in the wilderness. Time and events have altered its shape only to clothe it with a richer significance.

Will Great Britain decide wisely in the choice to which she is now put? Naturally, I do not speak of the Parliamentary future of the Home Rule Bill: that is safe. I have in mind rather that profound moral settlement, that generous reconciliation which we have seen in South Africa, and desire to see in Ireland. What of it? Did reason and the candid vision of things, as they are, control public affairs, there could be little doubt as to the issue in this choice between friendship and hatred, between the formula of freedom and that of domination. But, unhappily, we have no assurance that Philip sober rather than Philip drunk will sign the warrant. There exists in England, in respect of all things Irish, a monstrous residuum of prejudice. It lies ambushed in the blood even when it has been dismissed from the mind, and constitutes the real peril of the situation. No effort will be spared to reawaken it. The motto of militant Unionism has always been: When in doubt throw mud. Such a programme naturally begets a predilection for ditches, and when certain orators speak of the 'last ditch' they must be taken to mean that which has most mud in it. The old methods are already once more in operation. The wicked lying of previous campaigns no doubt cannot be repeated: bigotry will make no further experiments in Pigottry. But a resolute attempt, lavishly financed and directed by masters of the art of defamation, will be made to blacken Ireland. Every newspaper in every remotest country-town in England will be deluged with syndicated venom. The shopkeeper will wrap up his parcels in Orange posters, and the working-man will, I hope, light his pipe for years to come with pamphlets of the same clamant colour. Irishmen, or at all events persons born in Ireland, will be found to testify that they belong to a barbarous people which has never ceased from barbarism, and that they are not fit to govern themselves. Politicians who were never known to risk a five-pound note in helping to develop Ireland will toss down their fifties to help to defame her. Such is the outlook.

Against this campaign of malice, hatred, and all uncharitableness it is the duty of every good citizen to say his word, and in the following pages I say mine. This little book is not a compendium of facts, and so does not trench on the province of Mr Stephen Gwynn MP's admirable *Case for Home Rule*.[1] It does not discuss the details, financial or otherwise, of a statesmanlike settlement. Such suggestions as I had to make I have already made in *Home Rule Finance*, and the reader will find much ampler treatment of the whole subject in *The Framework of Home Rule*, by Mr Erskine Childers, and *Home Rule Problems*, edited by Mr Basil Williams.[2] In general, my aim has been to aid in humanising the Irish Question. The interpretation of various aspects of it, here offered, is intended to be not exhaustive but provocative, a mere set of shorthand rubrics any one of which might have been expanded into a chapter. Addressing the English reader with complete candour, I have attempted to recommend to him that method of approach, that mental attitude which alone can divest him of his preconceptions, and put him in rapport with the true spirit of the Ireland of actuality. To that end the various lines of discussion converge:

Chapter I is an outline of the pathology of the English mind in Ireland.

Chapters II and III present the history of Ireland as the epic, not of a futile and defeated, but of an indomitable and victorious people.

Chapter IV exhibits the Home Rule idea as a fundamental law of nature, human nature, and government.

Chapters V and VI contain a very brief account of the more obvious economic crimes and blunders of Unionism.

Chapter VII discusses the queer ideas of 'Ulster', and the queer reasons for the survival of these ideas.

Chapter VIII demonstrates that, as a mere matter of political technique, Home Rule must be conceded if any real government is ever to exist again, whether in Great Britain, in Ireland, or in the Empire.

Chapter IX dips into the future, and indicates that a Home Rule Ireland will have so much interesting work to do as to have no time for civil war or religious oppression.

Chapter X shows that everybody who values 'loyalty' must of necessity be a Home Ruler.

The only moral commended to the reader is that expressed by Browning in a firm and inevitable line, which has been disastrously forgotten in so many passages of English history:

> It's fitter being sane than mad.

I have tried also to convey to him, with what success others must judge, something of the 'pride and passion' of Irish nationality. That is, in truth, the dream that comes through the multitude of business. If you think that Home Rule is a little thing which must be done in a little way for little reasons, your feet are set on the path to failure. Home Rule is one of those fundamental reforms that are not achieved at all unless they are achieved greatly.

T. M. K.
December, 1911

CHAPTER I

An Exercise in Humility

In order to understand Ireland we must begin by understanding England. On no other terms will that complex of facts, memories, and passions, which is called the Irish Question, yield up its secret. 'You have always been', said a Lady Clanricarde to some English politician, 'like a high wall standing between us and the sun.' The phrase lives. It reveals in a flashlight of genius the historical relations of the two nations. It explains and justifies the principle adopted as the basis of this discussion, namely, that no examination of the Irish Problem is possible without a prior examination of the English mind. It used to be said that England dearly loved a Lord, a dictum which may have to be modified in the light of recent events. Far more than a Lord does the typical Englishman love a Judge, and the thought of acting as a Judge. Confronted with Ireland he says to himself: 'Here are these Irish people; some maintain that they are nice, others that they are nasty, but everybody agrees that they are queer. Very good. I will study them in a judicial spirit; I will weigh the evidence dispassionately, and give my decision. When it comes to action, I will play the honest broker between their contending parties.' Now this may be a very agreeable way of going about the business, but it is fatally unreal. Great Britain comes into court, she will be pained to hear, not as Judge but rather as defendant. She comes to answer the charge that, having seized Ireland as a 'trustee of civilisation', she has, either through incompetence or through dishonesty, betrayed her trust. We have a habit, in everyday life, of excusing the eccentricities of a friend or an enemy by the reflection that he is, after all, as God made him. Ireland is politically as Great Britain made her. Since the twelfth century, that is to say for a great part of the Middle Ages and for the whole of the modern period, the mind of England and not that of Ireland has been the dominant fact in Irish history.

This state of things – a paradox in action – carries with it certain metaphysical implications. The philosophers tell us that all morality centres in the maxim that others are to be treated as ends in themselves, and not as instruments to our ends. If they are right, then we must picture Ireland as the victim of a radical immoralism. We must think of her as a personality violated in its ideals, and arrested in its development. And, indeed, that is no bad way of thinking: it is the one formula which summarises the whole of her experience. But the phrasing is perhaps too high and absolute; and the decline and fall of Mr Balfour are a terrible example to those of us who, being young, might otherwise take metaphysics too solemnly. It will, therefore, at this stage be enough to repeat that, in contemplating the discontent and unrest which constitute the Irish difficulty, Great Britain is contemplating the work of her own hands, the creation of her own mind. For that reason we can make no progress until we ascertain what sort of mind we have to deal with.

I do not disguise from myself the extremely unpleasant nature of this inquiry. It is as if a counsel were to open his address by saying: 'Gentlemen of the Jury, before discussing the facts of the case I will examine briefly the mental flaws, gaps, kinks, and distortions of you twelve gentlemen.' There is, however, this difference. In the analysis upon which we are engaged the mental attitude of the jury is not merely a fact in the case, it is the whole case. Let me reinforce my weaker appeal by a passage from the wisest pen in contemporary English letters, that of Mr Chesterton. There is in his mere sanity a touch of magic so potent that, although incapable of dullness, he has achieved authority, and although convinced that faith is more romantic than doubt, or even sin, he has got himself published and read. Summarising the 'drift' of Matthew Arnold, Mr Chesterton observes:

> The chief of his services may perhaps be stated thus, that he disco
> vered (for the modern English) the purely intellectual importance of
> humility. He had none of that hot humility which is the fascination
> of saints and good men. But he had a cold humility which he had
> discovered to be a mere essential of the intelligence.

Such a humility, purely hygienic in character, is for Englishmen the beginning of wisdom on the Irish Question. It is the needle's eye by which alone they can enter a city otherwise forbidden to them. Let there be no misunderstanding. The attitude of mind commended to them is not without its agreeable features. Closely scrutinised, it is seen to be a sort of inverted vanity. The student begins by studying himself, an exercise in self-appraisal which need not by any means involve self-depreciation. What sort of a mind, then, is the English mind?

If there is anything in regard to which the love of friends corroborates the malice of enemies it is in ascribing to the English an individualism, hard-shelled beyond all human parallel. The Englishman's country is an impregnable island, his house is a castle, his temperament is a suit of armour. The function common to all three is to keep things out, and most admirably has he used them to that end. At first, indeed, he let everybody in; he had a perfect passion for being conquered, and Romans, Teutons, Danes,

and Normans in succession plucked and ate the apple of England.
But with the coming of age of that national consciousness, the
bonds of which have never been snapped, the English entered on
their lucky and courageous career of keeping things out. They
possess in London the only European capital that has never in the
modern period been captured by an invader. They withstood the
intellectual grandeur of Roman Law, and developed their own
medley of customs into the most eccentric and most equitable
system in the world. They kept out the Council of Trent, and the
Spanish Armada. They kept out the French Revolution, and
Napoleon. They kept out for a long time the Kantian philosophy,
Romanticism, Pessimism, Higher Criticism, German music,
French painting, and one knows not how many other of the
intellectual experiments that made life worth living, or not worth
living, to nineteenth-century Europe. Their insularity, spiritual as
well as geographical, has whetted the edge of a thousand flouts and
gibes. 'Those stupid French!' exclaims the sailor, as reported by
De Morgan: 'Why do they go on calling a cabbage a *shoe* when they
must know that it is a *cabbage*?' This was in general the attitude of
what Mr Newbolt has styled the 'Island Race' when on its travels.
Everybody has laughed at the comedy of it, but no one has sufficiently applauded its success. The English tourist declined to be at
the trouble of speaking any foreign tongue whatsoever; instantly
every hotel and restaurant on the Continent was forced to learn
English. He refused to read their books; a Leipsic firm at once
started to publish his own, and sold him his six-shilling Clapham
novels in Lucerne for two francs. He dismissed with indignation
the idea of breakfasting on a roll, and bacon and eggs were added
unto him. In short, by a straightforward policy of studying nobody
else, he compelled everybody else to study him.

Now it is idle to deny this performance the applause which it
plainly deserves. The self-evolution of England, as it may perhaps

be called, in its economic, political, and literary life, offers an admirable model of concentration and energy. Even where it is a case of obtuseness to other civilisations, at least as high but of a different type, the verdict cannot be wholly unfavourable. The Kingdom of Earth is to the thick-skinned, and bad manners have a distinct vital value. A man, too sensitive to the rights and the charms of others, is in grave danger of futility. Either he will become a dilettante, which is the French way, or he will take to drink and mystical nihilism, a career very popular in Russian fiction. Bad manners have indeed a distinct ethical value. We all experience moods in which we politely assent to the thing that is not, because of the fatigue of fighting for the thing that is. A temperament such as has been delineated is therefore, as human types go, an excellent type. But it has its peculiar perils. To ignore the point of view of those in whose country you eat, drink, sleep, and sight-see may breed only minor discords, and after all you will pay for your manners in your bill. But to ignore the point of view of those whose country you govern may let loose a red torrent of tragedy. Such a temper of mind may, at the first touch of resistance, transform your stolid, laudable, laughable Englishman into the beastliest of tyrants. It may drive him into a delirium of cruelty and injustice. It may sweep away, in one ruin of war, wealth, culture, and the whole fabric of civilisation. It may darken counsel, and corrupt thought. In fact, it may give you something very like the history of the English in Ireland.

Now it is not denied that most Englishmen believe the English mind to be incapable of such excesses. This, they say, is the Russian in Warsaw, the Austrian in Budapest, the Belgian in the Congo, the blind fool-fury of the Seine. But it is not the English way. Nor is it suggested that this illusion is sheer and mere hypocrisy. It is simply an hallucination of jingoism. Take a trivial instance in point. We have all read in the newspapers derisive accounts of disorderly scenes in the French Chamber or the Austrian Reichstag; we all know the complacent sigh with which England is wont on such occasions to thank God that she is not as one of those. Does anybody think that this attitude will be at all modified by recent occurrences at Westminster? By no means. Lord Hugh Cecil, his gibbering and gesticulating quite forgotten, will be assuring the House next year that the Irish are so deficient in self-restraint as to be unfit for Home Rule. Mr Smith will be deploring that intolerant temper which always impels a Nationalist to shout down, and not to argue down an opponent. Mr Walter Long will be vindicating the cause of law and order in one sentence, and inciting 'Ulster' to bloodshed in the next. This is not hypocrisy, it is genius. It is also, by the way, the genesis of the Irish Question. If anyone is disposed to underrate the mad passions of which race hatred can slip the leash, let him recall the crucial examples which we have had in our own time. We have in our own time seen Great Britain inflamed by two frenzies – against France, and against the Boer Republics. In the history of public opinion there are no two chapters more discreditable. In the days of Fashoda the Frenchman was a degenerate *tigre-singe*, the sworn enemy of religion and soap. He had contributed nothing to civilisation except a loathsome science of sensuality, and the taint of decay was in his bones. In the days of Spion Kop the Boer was an unlaundered savage, fit only to be a target for pig-stickers. His ignorance seemed the most appalling thing in the world until one remembered his hypocrisy and his cowardice. The newspaper which led the campaign of denigration against France has come to another view. Its proprietor now divides his time between signing £10,000 cheques for triumphant French aviators, and delivering speeches in which their nation is hailed as the pioneer of all great ideas. As regards the Boers, the same reversal of the verdict of ten years ago has taken place. The crowd which in 1900 asked only for a sour apple-tree on which to hang General Botha, adopts him in 1911 as the idol of the Coronation. At this progress towards sanity we must all rejoice. But most of all we have to ask that these two sinister pageants of race hatred shall not be suffered to dissolve without leaving some wrack of wisdom behind. Writers on psychology have made many studies of what they call the collective illusion. This strange malady, which consists in all the world seeing something which in fact does not exist, wrought more potently on the mind of England than did reason and justice in the Home Rule controversies of 1886 and 1893. What has occurred may recur. And since we are to speak here with all the candour of private conversation I confess that I cannot devise or imagine any specific against such a recurrence except an exercise in humility of the kind suggested by Mr Chesterton. My own argument in that direction is perhaps compromised by the fact that I am an Irishman. Let us therefore fall back on other testimony. Out of the cloud of witnesses let us choose two or three, and in the first place M. Alfred Fouillée. M. Fouillée is a Platonist – the last Platonist in Europe – and consequently an amiable man. He is universally regarded as the leader of philosophy in France, a position not in the least shaken by Bergson's brief authority. In a charming and lucid study of the 'Psychology of the Peoples of Europe' Fouillée has many pages that might serve for an introduction to the Irish Question.[3] The point of interest in his analysis is this: he exhibits Irish history as a tragedy of character, a tragedy which flows with sad, inevitable logic from a certain weakness which he notes, not in the Irish, but in the English character.

'In the eyes of the English', says Taine who had studied them so minutely, 'there is but one reasonable civilisation, namely their own. Every other way of living is that of inferior beings, every other religion is extravagant.' So that, one might add, the Englishman is doubly personal, first as an individual and again as a member of the most highly individualised of nations. The moment the national interest is involved all dissensions cease, there is on the scene but one single man, one single Englishman, who shrinks from no expedient that may advance his ends. Morality for him reduces itself to one precept: Safeguard at any cost the interest of England.

Like all foreigners he takes Ireland as the one conspicuous and flaming failure of England. In that instance she has muddled, as usual, but she has not muddled through.

The Anglo–Saxons, those great colonisers of far–off lands, have in their own United Kingdom succeeded only in inflicting a long martyrdom on Ireland. The insular situation of England had for pendant the insular situation of Ireland; the two islands lie there face to face. The English and the Irish, although intellectually very much alike, have preserved different characters. And this difference cannot be due essentially to the racial element, for nearly half Ireland is Germanic. It is due to traditions and customs developed by English oppression.

Having summarised the main lines of British policy in Ireland, he concludes:

It is not easy to detect here any sign of the 'superiority of the Anglo–Saxons'.

With Fouillée we may associate Emile Boutmy. In his 'Political Psychology of the English'[4] he declares that the haughty, taciturn, solitary, unassimilative temperament of England, so admirable from the point of view of self-development, shows its worst side and comes to a malign florescence in the history of Ireland. It explains why the relations of Ireland with England have been, for so many centuries, those of a captive with his jailer, those of a victim with his torturer.

I pass over De Beaumont, Von Raumer, Perraud, Paul-Dubois, Filon, Bonn. The considerations already adduced ought to be enough to lead the English reader to certain conclusions which are fundamental. For the sake of clearness they may be repeated in all their nudity:

England has failed in Ireland.

Her failure has been due to defects of her own character, and limitations of her outlook. The same defects which corrupted her policy in the past distort her vision in the present.

Therefore, if she is to understand and to solve the Irish Question, she must begin by breaking the hard shell of her individualism, and trying to think herself into the skin, the soul, and the ideals of the Irish nation.

Now the English reader is after all human. If he has endured so far the outrage on his most sacred prejudices perpetrated in this chapter he must at this moment be hot with resentment. He must feel as if, proposing to his imagination Pear de Melba, he had in truth swallowed sand. Let me end with a more comfortable word. We have seen that Irish history is what the dramatists call an internal tragedy, the secular disclosure and slow working-out of certain flaws in the English character. I am not to be understood as ascribing horns to England and a halo to Ireland. We Irish are not only imperfect but even modest; for every beam that we detect in another eye we are willing to confess a mote in our own. The English on the other hand have been not monsters or demons, but men unstrung.

> In tragic life, God wot,
> No villain need be, passions spin the plot;
> We are betrayed by what is false within.

Least of all am I to be understood as ascribing to modern Englishmen any sort of planned, aforethought malice in regard to Ireland. It is what Bacon might have called a mere idol of the platform to suppose that they are filled with a burning desire to oppress Ireland. The dream of their lives is to ignore her, to eliminate from their calculations this variable constant which sheds bewilderment upon every problem. Could they but succeed in that, a very Sabbath of peace would have dawned for them. The modern Englishman is too much worried to plan the oppression of anybody. 'Did you ever', asked Lord Salisbury on a remembered occasion, 'have a boil on your neck?' To the Englishman of 1911 – that troubled man whose old self-sufficiency has in our own time been shattered beyond repair by Boer rifles, German shipyards, French aeroplanes – Ireland is the boil on the neck of his political system. It is the one *péché de jeunesse* of his nation that will not sleep in the grave of the past. Like the ghost in *Hamlet* it pursues and plagues him without respite. Shunned on the battlements it invades his most private chamber, or, finding him in talk with friends, shames and scares him with subterranean mutterings. Is there no way out of a situation so troublesome and humiliating?

There is. Ireland cannot be ignored, but she can easily be appeased. The boil is due to no natural and incurable condition. It is the direct result of certain artificial ligatures and compressions; remove these and it disappears. This spectre haunts the conscience of England to incite her not to a deed of blood but to a deed of justice; every wind is favourable and every omen. It is, indeed, true that if she is to succeed, England must do violence to certain prejudices which now afflict her like a blindness; she must deal with us as a man with men. But is not the Kingdom of Heaven taken by violence?

CHAPTER II

History
(a) Coloured

Mendacity follows the flag. There never yet was an invader who did not, in obedience to a kindly human instinct, lie abundantly respecting the people whose country he had invaded. The reason is very plain. In all ages men delight to acquire property by expedients other than that of honest labour. In the period of private war the most obvious alternative to working is fighting, or hiring servants to fight; the sword is mightier than the spade. If we add that an expedition into a foreign country offers the additional advantages of escape from your exacting creditors, and your still more exacting king, we have something very like the economics of the Invasion of Anywhere in early feudal times. Had the leaders of these invasions, or rather their clerkly secretaries, written the plain tale of their doings they would have left some such record as this: 'There were we, a band of able-bodied, daring, needy men. Our only trade was war; our only capital our suits of armour, our swords and battle-axes. We heard that there was good land and rich booty to be had in Anywhere; we went and fought for it. Our opponents were brave men, too, but badly organised. In some places we won. There we substituted our own law for the queer sort of law under which these people had lived; when they resisted too strongly we had, of course, no option but to kill them. In other places we got mixed up completely by alliances and marriages with the old stock, and lived most agreeably with them. In others again the natives killed us, and remained in possession. Such was the Invasion of Anywhere.'

But (I had almost said unhappily) the invaders were not content with having swords, they had also consciences. They were Christians, and thought it necessary to justify themselves before the High Court of Christian Europe. Consequently the clerks had to write up the record in quite a different fashion. They discovered that their bluff, hard-bitten, rather likeable employers, scarcely one of whom could read or write, had really invaded Anywhere as the trustees of civilisation. Now it may be said in general – and the observation extends to our own time – that the moment an invader discovers that he is the trustee of civilisation he is irretrievably lost to the truth. He is forced by his own pose to become not an unprincipled liar, but that much more disgusting object, a liar on principle. He is bound, in order to legitimise his own position, to prove that 'the natives' are savages, living in a morass of nastiness and ignorance. All facts must be adapted to this conclusion. The clerks, having made this startling discovery, went on to supplement it by the further discovery that their masters had invaded Anywhere in order to please the Pope, and introduce true religion. This second rôle completes the dedication of the invaders on the altar of mendacity. It was Leo XIII himself who, with that charming humour of his, deprecated the attitude of certain *a priori* historians who, said he, if they were writing the Gospel story would, in their anxiety to please the Pope, probably suppress the denial of Peter.

These things which might have happened anywhere did, in fact, happen in Ireland. Out of the footprints of the invaders there sprang up a legion of fictionists, professional cooks of history. Beginning with Giraldus Cambrensis they ought to have ended, but, as we shall see, did not end with Froude. The significance of these mercenaries of literature can hardly be exaggerated; it is not too much to say that they found Ireland a nation, and left her a question. It is not at all that they put on record the thing that was not as regards the events of their own period. That might be and has been amended by the labours of impartial scholarship. The real crime of the fabulists lies in this, that their tainted testimony constituted for honest Englishmen the only information about Ireland easily obtainable. The average Englishman (that is to say, the forty millions of him who do not read learned books of any kind) comes to the consideration of contemporary Ireland with a vision distorted almost beyond hope of cure. The treasured lies of seven hundred years are in his heart to-day. For time runs against the cause of truth as well as with it. Once create a Frankenstein of race hatred, and he will gather strength in going. The chronicler's fable of this century becomes the accredited historical fact of the next. Give it what billiard-players call 'legs' enough and it will mature into a tradition, a proverb, a spontaneous instinct. There is a whole department of research concerned with the growth of myths, stage by stage, from a little nebulous blotch into a peopled world of illusion. The strange evolution there set forth finds an exact parallel in the development of English opinion on Ireland. And, indeed, the more you study 'the Irish Question', as it is envisaged by the ruling mind of Great Britain, the more conscious are you of moving in the realm not of reason but of mythology.

All this will seem obvious even to the point of weariness. But it is of interest as furnishing a clue to the English attitude towards Irish history; I should rather say attitudes, for there are two. The first is that of the Man of Feeling. His mode of procedure recalls inevitably an exquisite story which is to be found somewhere in Rousseau. During country walks, Jean Jacques tells us, his father would suddenly say: 'My son, we will speak of your dear, dead mother.' And Jean Jacques was expected to reply: 'Wait, then, a moment, my dear father. I will first search for my handkerchief, for I perceive that we are going to weep.' In precisely such a mood of deliberate melancholy does the sentimentalist address himself to the Confiscations and the Penal Laws. He is ready to praise without stint any Irish leader who happens to be sufficiently dead. He is ready to confess that all his own British forerunners were abominable blackguards. He admits, not only with candour but even with a certain enthusiastic remorse, that England oppressed Ireland in every phase of their relations. Then comes the conclusion. So terrible have been the sins of his fathers that he feels bound to make restitution. And in order to make restitution, to be kind and helpful and remedial, he must retain the management of Irish affairs in his benevolent hands. In order to expiate the crimes of the past he must repeat the basal blunder that was the cause and source of them. For this kind of sympathy we have only to say, in a somewhat vulgar phrase, that we have no use whatever. The Englishman who 'sympathises' with Ireland is lost.

But the more general attitude differs widely from this. Confronting us with a bluff and not unkindly demeanour, worthy of the nation that invented cold baths as a tonic against all spiritual anguish, the practical, modern Englishman speaks out his mind in straight-flung words and few. 'You fellows,' he says, 'brood too much over the past. After all, this is the twentieth century, not the twelfth. What does it matter whether my ancestors murdered yours or not? Both would be dead now in any event. What does it matter whether yours were the saints and men of letters and mine the savages, or whether the boot was on the other leg? That's all over and done with. Imitate me. Let bygones be bygones.'

Now this is, in some respects, the authentic voice of health. Undoubtedly the most characteristic thing about the past is that it is not present, and to lavish on it too tragic and intense a devotion is to love death more than life. And yet our bluff Englishman can

learn in two words how it comes about that his invitation represents a demand for the impossible. In the first place, the bygones
have not gone by. Our complaint is made not against the crimes of
his fathers, who are dead, but against the crimes of himself and his
fellows, who are alive. We denounce not the repealed Penal Laws
but the unrepealed Act of Union. If we recall to the memory of
England the systematic baseness of the former, it is in order to
remind her that she once thought them right, and now confesses
that they were cruelly wrong. We Irish are realists, and we hold the
problems of the present as of more account than any agonies or
tyrannies of the past. But our realism has the human touch in
it, and that constitutes the second impossibility in the invitation
tendered us. *Que messieurs les assassins commencent!* The anti-Irish
legend is not dead nor even sleeping, nor are the resources of
calumny yet exhausted. An instance is immediately at hand. I have,
at this moment, on my desk a volume lately issued – *The School
History of England*. It is published by the Clarendon Press, Oxford;
Mr Rudyard Kipling contributes twenty-three pieces of verse, and
a Mr C. R. L. Fletcher, whose qualifications are not stated, appears
to be responsible for the prose.[5] The book has been praised in most
of the papers, and it will no doubt go far. This is the picture of the
coming to Ireland of the Cymro-Frankish adventurers which its
pages will imprint on the minds of the youth of England:

> One event of his reign (Henry II's) must not be forgotten, his visit to
> Ireland in 1171–2. St Patrick, you may have heard, had banished the
> snakes from that island, but he had not succeeded in banishing the
> murderers and thieves who were worse than many snakes. In spite of
> some few settlements of Danish pirates and traders on the eastern
> coast, Ireland had remained purely Celtic and purely a pasture country.
> All wealth was reckoned in cows; Rome had never set foot there, so
> there was a king for every day in the week, and the sole amusement of

such persons was to drive off each other's cows and to kill all who resisted. In Henry II's time this had been going on for at least seven hundred years, and during the seven hundred that have followed much the same thing would have been going on, if the English Government had not occasionally interfered.

The English whom Henry II left behind him soon became 'as wild and barbarous as the Irishmen themselves'.

Oxford, the home of so many other lost causes, apparently aspires to be also the home of the lost cause of mendacity. The forcible-feeble malice of Mr Fletcher calls for no serious discussion; submit it to any continental scholar, to any honest British scholar, and he will ask contemptuously, though perhaps with a little stab of pain, how the name of Oxford comes to be associated with such wicked absurdities. Every other reference to Ireland is marked by the same scientific composure and balanced judgment. And this document, inspired by race hatred, and apparently designed to propagate race hatred, is offered to the youth of these countries as an aid towards the consolidation of the Empire. It is a case not merely of the poisoning of a well, but of the poisoning of a great river at its source. The force of cowardice can no farther go. So long as it goes thus far, so long as the Froudes find Fletchers to echo them, Irishmen will inevitably 'brood over the past'. We do not share the cult of ancestor-worship, but we hold the belief that the Irish nation, like any other, is an organism endowed with a life in some sort continuous and repetitive of its origins. To us it does matter something whether our forerunners were turbulent savages, destitute of all culture, or whether they were valiant, immature men labouring through the twilight of their age towards that dawn which does not yet flush our own horizon. But we are far from wishing that dead centuries should be summoned back to wake old bitterness that ought also to be dead. Hand history over to the scholars, if you will; let it be marshalled as a multitudinous and coloured pageant, to incite imaginations and inspire literature. Such is our desire, but when we read the clotted nonsense of persons like Mr Fletcher we can only repeat: *Que messieurs les assassins commencent!*

For the purpose of this inquiry it is inevitable that some brief account should be rendered of the past relations between England and Ireland. The reader need not shrink back in alarm; it is not proposed to lead him by the reluctant nose through the whole maze and morass of Irish history. The past is of value to political realists only in that residue of it which survives, namely, the wisdom which it ought to have taught us. Englishmen are invited to consider the history of Ireland solely from that point of view. They are prayed to purge themselves altogether of pity, indignation, and remorse; these are emotions far too beneficent to waste on things outside the ambit of our own immediate life. If they are wise they will come to Irish history as to a school, and they will learn one lesson that runs through it like the refrain of a ballad. A very simple lesson it is, just this: Ireland cannot be put down. Ireland always has her way in the end. If the opposite view is widely held the explanation lies on the surface. Two causes have co-operated to produce the illusion. Everybody agrees that Great Britain has acted in a most black-guardly fashion towards Ireland; everybody assumes that blackguard-ism always succeeds in this world, therefore Ireland is a failure. The only flaw in this syllogism is that it is in direct conflict with every known fact. For the rest we have to thank or blame the sentimentalism of Mr Matthew Arnold. His proud but futile Celts who 'went down to battle but always fell' have been mistaken for the Irish of actual history. The truth is, of course, that the phrase is in the grand manner of symbolism. When Ecclesiastes laments that the eye is not filled with seeing nor the ear with hearing we do not argue him deaf and blind; we take his words as a proclamation of that famine and fierce appetite of the spirit which has created all the higher religions. Ireland agrees with Ecclesiastes. Perceiving that there is in matter no integral and permanent reality she cannot be content with material victories; her poets are subtle in what a French writer styles the innuendoes by which the soul makes its enormous claims. The formula of her aspiration has been admirably rendered by the late Mrs Nora Chesson:

> He follows after shadows when all your chase is done;
> He follows after shadows, the King of Ireland's son.

Were I to read the poem, of which these lines are the motif, to certain genial Englishmen of my acquaintance they would observe that the gentleman in question was a 'queer cove, staying up late at night and catching cold, and that no doubt there was a woman in the case'. But these are considerations a little remote from the daily dust of politics. In the sense in which every life is a failure, and the best life the worst failure, Ireland is a failure. But in every other sense, in all that touches the fathomable business of daylight, she has been a conspicuous success.

A certain type of fanaticism is naive enough to regard the intercourse of England with Ireland as that of a superior with an inferior race. This is the sanction invoked to legitimise every adventure in invasion and colonisation. M. Jules Hormand [*sic*], who has attempted, in his recent book, *Domination et Colonisation*,[6] to formulate a theory of the whole subject, touches bed-rock when he writes:

> We must then accept as our point of departure the principle that there is a hierarchy of races and of civilisations, and that we belong to the higher race and civilisation. . . . The essential legitimation of conquest is precisely this conviction of our own superiority. . . . Nations which

do not hold this belief, because incapable of such sincerity towards themselves, should not attempt to conquer others.

The late Lord Salisbury was grasping at such a justification when he likened the Irish to Hottentots; it would be a justification of a kind if it chanced to be validated by the facts. But it does not. There is so much genuine humour in the comparison that, for my part, I am unable to take offence at it. I look at the lathe painted to look like iron, and I set over against him Parnell. That is enough; the lathe is smashed to fragments amid the colossal laughter of the gods. The truth is that in every shock and conflict of Irish civilisation with English, it is the latter that has given way. The obscuration of this obvious fact is probably to be ascribed to the military successes of the Norman, or rather the Cymro–Frankish invaders. If we were the higher race why did we not put them out? Replying on the same plane of thought we observe that if they were the higher race they would have put us down. But a more detailed assignment of qualities between the two peoples is possible. In general it may be said that the two stood on much the same level of mentality, but that they had specialised on different subjects, the Normans on war and politics, the Irish on culture. Of the many writers who help us to reconstruct the period we ought to signalise one, Mrs A. S. Green, who to a rare scholarship adds something rarer, the genius of common sense. This is not the place in which to recall the whole substance of her *Making of Ireland and its Undoing* and her *Irish Nationality*; but from borrowings thence and elsewhere we can piece together a plain tale of that first chapter of the Irish Question.[7]

CHAPTER III

History

(b) Plain

In those days war was the most lucrative industry open to a young man of breeding, courage, and ability. Owners of capital regarded it as a sound investment. What Professor Oman tells us of the Normans in 1066 was equally true of them in 1169:

> Duke William had undertaken his expedition not as a mere feudal lord of the barons of Normandy but rather as the managing director of a great joint-stock company for the conquest of England, in which not only his own subjects but hundreds of adventurers, poor and rich, from all parts of Western Europe had taken shares.

The Normans, then, came to Ireland with their eyes on three objects. In the first place, property. This was to be secured in the case of each individual adventurer by the overthrow of some individual Irish chieftain. It necessitated war in the shape of a purely local, and indeed personal grapple. In the second place, plunder. This was to be secured by raids, incursions, and temporary alliances. In the third place, escape from the growing power and exactions of the Crown. This was to be secured geographically by migration to Ireland, and politically by delaying, resolutely if discreetly, the extension in that country of the over-lordship of the

King. Herein lies the explanation of the fact that for three and a half centuries the English penetration into Ireland is a mere chaos of private appetites and egotisms. The invaders, as we have said, were specialists in war, and in the unification of states through war. This they had done for England; this they failed to do for Ireland. The one ingredient which, if dropped into the seething cauldron of her life, must have produced the definite crystallisation of a new nationality, complete in structure and function, was not contributed. True, the Cymro-Franks proved themselves strong enough in arms to maintain their foothold; if that physical test is enough to establish their racial superiority then let us salute Mr Jack Johnson as Zarathustra, the superman. But in their one special and characteristic task they failed lamentably. Instead of conquest and consolidation they gave us mere invasion and disturbance. The disastrous rôle played by them has been unfolded by many interpreters of history, by none with a more vivid accuracy than we find in the pages of M. Paul-Dubois:

Had Ireland been left to herself she would, in all human probability, have succeeded, notwithstanding her decadence, in establishing political unity under a military chief. Had the country been brought into peaceful contact with continental civilisation, it must have advanced along the path of modern progress. Even if it had been conquered by a powerful nation, it would at least have participated in the progress of the conquering power. But none of these things happened. England, whose political and social development had been hastened by the Norman Conquest, desired to extend her influence to Ireland. 'She wished,' as Froude strangely tells us, 'to complete the work of civilisation happily begun by the Danes.' But in actual fact she only succeeded in trammelling the development of Irish society, and maintaining in the country an appalling condition of decadent stagnation, as the result of three centuries and a half of intermittent invasions, never followed by conquest.[8]

On the other hand the triumph of Irish culture was easy and absolute. Ireland, unvisited by the legions and the law of Rome, had evolved a different vision of the life of men in community, or, in other words, a different idea of the State. Put very briefly the difference lay in this. The Romans and their inheritors organised for purposes of war and order, the Irish for purposes of culture. The one laid the emphasis on police, the other on poets. But for a detailed exposition of the contrast I must send the reader to Mrs Green's *Irish Nationality*. In a world in which right is little more than a secretion of might, in which, unless a strong man armed keeps house, his enemies enter in, the weakness of the Gaelic idea is obvious. But the Roman pattern too had a characteristic vice which has led logically in our own time to a monstrous and sinister growth of armaments.

To those who recognise in this deification of war the blackest menace of our day the vision of a culture State is not without charm. The shattering possibilities enfolded in it would have fevered Nietzsche and fascinated Renan. But, be that as it may, Ireland played Cleopatra to the Antony of the invaders. Some of them, indeed, the 'garrison' pure and simple, had all their interests centred not only in resisting but in calumniating her. But the majority yielded gaily to her music, her poetry, her sociability, that magical quality of hers which the Germans call *Gemütlichkeit*. In a few centuries a new and enduring phrase had designated them as more Irish than the Irish themselves. So far as any superiority of civilisation manifests itself in this first period it is altogether on the side of Ireland. This power of assimilation has never decayed. There never was a nation, not even the United States, that so subdued and re-fashioned those who came to her shores, that so wrought them into her own blood and tissue. The Norman baron is transformed in a few generations into an Irish chieftain, and as often as not into an Irish 'rebel'. The Jacobite planter of the first decade of the seventeenth century is in the fifth decade found in arms against Cromwell; the Cromwellian settler is destined in turn to shed his blood for James II and Catholicity. Protestant colonists who, in the early eighteenth century, enforce and defend the abominable Penal Laws, will in 1782 demand, with drawn swords, that henceforth there shall be no longer a Protestant colony but in its place an Irish nation. The personal history of the captains of the Irish cause in modern times is no less remarkable. O'Connell begins his public career in the Yeomanry called out to put down the insurrectionary movement of Emmet. Isaac Butt comes first into note as the orator of the Orange Party in Dublin. Parnell himself steps out of a Tory milieu and tradition into the central tumult of agitation. Wave after incoming wave of them, her conquerors were conquered. 'Once again', cried Parnell in the last public utterance of his life, 'I am come to cast myself into the deep sea of the love of my people.' In that deep sea a hundred diverse currents of blood have met and mingled; they have lost their individual drift to become part of the strong tide of national consciousness and national unity. If Irish history is to be regarded as a test of racial superiority then Ireland emerges with the crown and garlands of victory. We came, we the invaders, to dominate, and we remained to serve. For Ireland has signed us with the oil and chrism of her human sacrament, and even though we should deny the faith with our lips she would hold our hearts to the end.

But let us translate her triumph into more concrete speech. The essential lesson of experience, then, is that no device, plan, or policy adopted by England for the subjugation of Ireland has ever been anything except an abject failure. And the positive of this negative is that every claim that ever formed part of the national programme of Ireland has won its way against all enmities. No plough to which she ever put her hand has been turned back or stayed eternally in mid-furrow. It does not matter what period you call to the witness-box; the testimony is uniform and unvarying. Until Tudor times, as has been noted, there cannot be said to have been in any strict sense an English policy in Ireland; there was only a scuffle of appetites. In so far as there was a policy it consisted of sporadic murder for the one half, and for the other of an attempt to prevent all intercourse that might lead to amalgamation between the two peoples. The Statute of Kilkenny – which is, all things considered, more important than the Kilkenny cats though not so well known in England – made it a capital offence for a settler to marry an Irishwoman or to adopt the Irish language, law, or costume. The Act no doubt provided a good many ruffians with legal and even ecclesiastical fig-leaves with which to cover their ruffianism, and promoted among the garrison such laudable objects as rape and assassination. But as a breakwater between the two races it did not fulfil expectation. The Statute was passed in 1367: and two centuries later Henry VIII was forced to appoint as his Deputy the famous Garrett Fitzgerald whose life was a militant denial of every clause and letter of it. With the Tudors, after some diplomatic preliminaries, a very clear and business-like policy was developed. Seeing that the only sort of quiet Irishman known to contemporary science was a dead Irishman, English Deputies and Governors were instructed to pacify Ireland by slaughtering or starving the entire population. The record of their conscientious effort to obey these instructions may be studied in any writer of the period, or in any historian, say Mr Froude. For Mr Froude, in his pursuit of the picturesque, was always ready to resort to the most extreme measures; he sometimes even went so far as to tell the truth. The noblest and ablest English minds lent their aids. Sir Walter Raleigh and Edmund Spenser were both rather circumam-bulatory on paper; the work of each is a long monotone broken by two or three exquisite immortalities. But they were both as concise in action as an Elizabethan headsman. Sir Walter helped Lord

Grey, the recognised pattern in those days of the Christian gentle-man, to put to death seven hundred prisoners-of-war at Smerwick. Spenser, being no soldier, leaned rather to famine. In his famous book he recommends the destruction of crops, houses, cattle, and all necessaries of life so that the Irish should 'soon be compelled to devour each other'.[9] The Commanders-in-Chief and the Deputies specialised in poison, as became men whose wealth and learning enabled them to keep in touch with the Italian Renaissance. Bluff, straightforward troopers like Mountjoy, Malby, Wilmot, Bagenal, Chichester, and the rest, not pretending to such refinements, did their best in the way of hanging, stabbing, and burning. In those days as well as ours the children had their Charter. 'Nits', said the trustees of civilisation, 'will grow to lice'. And so they tossed them on the points of their swords, thus combining work with play, or fed them on the roast corpses of their relatives, and afterwards strangled them with tresses of their mother's hair.

I do not recall these facts in order to show that Elizabethan policy was a riot of blackguardism. That is obvious, and it is irre-levant. I mention them in order to show that the blackguardism under review was an unrelieved failure. At one time, indeed, it seemed to have succeeded.

'Ireland, brayed as in a mortar, to use Sir John Davies' phrase,' writes M. Paul-Dubois, 'at last submitted. In the last years of the century half the population had perished. Elizabeth reigned over corpses and ashes. *Hibernia Pacata* – Ireland is "pacified".'

The blunder discloses itself at a glance. Only half the popu-lation had perished; there were still alive, according to the most probable estimate, quite two hundred thousand Irishmen. The next generation helps to illustrate not only the indestructibility of Ireland, but her all but miraculous power of recuperation. So abundant are the resources of his own vitality that, as Dr Moritz Bonn declares, an Irish peasant can live where a continental goat would starve. And not having read Malthus – Mr Malthus at that time being even less readable than since – the Irish remnant proceeded to develop anew into a nation. In forty years it was marching behind that *beau chevalier* Owen Roe O'Neill to battle and victory. O'Neill, a general famous through Europe, the one man who might have measured equal swords with Cromwell, was removed by poison, and then came the massacres. In eleven years, Sir William Petty assures us, 616,000 out of a total population of 1,466,000 perished by the sword or by starvation. For the remainder the policy of root and branch extermination was abandoned in favour of a policy of State-aided migration and emigration. As an alternative to hell the Irish were deported to Connaught or the Barbadoes. Henceforth there were to be three provinces of loyal English, and one of rebelly Irish. This again was not a radiant success. The transformation of the Cromwellian settler has been indicated; if you were to search for him to-day you would probably find him President of the local branch of the United Irish League. The story repeats itself period after period. The Penal Laws did not protestantise Ireland. The eighteenth century may be said to mark the lowest ebb of national life, but the tide was to turn. After Aughrim and the Boyne, the new device of England was to sacrifice everything to the 'garrison'. 'Protestant Ireland', as Grattan put it, 'knelt to England on the necks of her countrymen.' In one aspect the garrison were tyrants; in another they were slaves. They were at once oppressors and oppressed. There was a sort of 'deal' between them and the English Government by which the public welfare was to be sacrificed to the English Government, the Irish Catholics to the 'garrison'. A vile programme, but subtle and adroit, it bore its unnatural fruit of legislation, passed by the Westminster Parliament and the Dublin Garrison Parliament alike, for the destruction of every manufacturing and commercial interest in Ireland that was thought to conflict with a similar interest in England. But another debacle has to be chronicled. Out of the very baseness of this regime a new patriotism was begotten. The garrison, awakening abruptly to the fact that it had no country, determined to invent one; and there was brought to birth that modern Ireland, passionate for freedom, which has occupied the stage ever since. In our own time it has knit, as a fractured limb knits, into one tissue with the tradition of the Gaelic peasantry. Hanging and burning, torture and oppression, poison and Penal Laws, bribes and blackguardism so far from exterminating the Irish people actually hammered them into a nation, one and indestructible, proud of its past and confident of its future.

Take instances still more recent and particular – the struggle for religious freedom or the struggle for the land. Catholic emancipation is a leading case: obstinacy against obstinacy, the No! of England against the Yes! of Ireland, and the former sprawling in the ditch at the end of the tussle. 'The Law', ran the dictum of an eighteenth-century Lord Chancellor, 'does not suppose any such person to exist as an Irish Roman Catholic.' At this moment a Catholic holds the seals and purse of the Chancellorship. Never did ministers swallow their own stubborn words more incontinently than did Peel and Wellington. So late as 1828 Peel was loudly declaring that the continuance of these bars, which excluded the Catholics from the acquisition of political power, was necessary for the maintenance of the Constitution and the safety of the Church, and Wellington was echoing his words. A year later, utterly defeated by O'Connell, Peel was introducing the Catholic Relief Bill in the Commons. Wellington had it for his task to induce, or rather frighten the king to assent. Ireland not only emancipated the Catholics, she went on to emancipate the Dissenters, a service of freedom of conscience which is too often forgotten.

The Tithe System was similarly declared to be part of the fabric of the Constitution, to be upheld at the point of the bayonet.

Scythe in hand, the Irish peasant proclaimed that it must go. It went. Still more fundamental was the existence of the Protestant Established Church. To touch it was to lay hands on the Ark. Orange orators threatened civil war; two hundred thousand Ulstermen were to shoulder their Minie Rifles, and not merely slaughter the Catholics but even depose Queen Victoria.

Ireland said that the Establishment too must go; and, with the echoed menace of Fenianism ringing in his ears, Mr Gladstone hauled down the official blazon of Ascendancy. 'Ulster' did not fight. But the fierce struggle for the land affords the crucial test. Landlordism of that most savage type which held for its whole gospel that a man may do what he likes with his own was conceived to be the very corner-stone of British rule in Ireland. It controlled Parliament, the judiciary, the schools, the Press, and possessed in the Royal Irish Constabulary an incomparable watch-dog. It had resisted the criticism and attack loosened against it by the scandal of the Great Famine. Then suddenly Ireland took the business in hand. On a certain day in October 1879, some thirty men met in a small hotel in Dublin and, under the inspiration of Michael Davitt, founded the Land League. To the programme then formulated, the expropriation of the landlords at twenty years' purchase of their rents, England as usual said No! The proposal was thundered against as confiscation, communism, naked and shameful. To any student, with patience sufficient for the task, the contemporary files of such journals as the *Times* will furnish an exquisite chapter in the literature of obtuseness. England sustained her No! with batons, bullets, plank-beds, Coercion courts, and an occasional halter; Ireland her Yes! with 'agitation'. Is it necessary to ask who won? Is it necessary to trace step by step the complete surrender of the last ditchers of those days? The fantastic and wicked dreams of the agitators have in thirty years translated themselves into Statute Law and solid fact. An English statesman of the period, say

Mr Balfour or Mr Wyndham, is fortunate if, with a few odd rags pilfered from the Land League wardrobe, he can conceal from history his utter poverty of ideas.

This, then, is the essential wisdom of Irish history: Ireland has won all along the line. The Normans did not normanise her. The Tudors did not exterminate her. She has undone the Confiscations, and drawn a cancelling pen through the Penal Laws. The Act of Union, so far from suppressing her individuality or overwhelming it, has actually brought it to that full self-consciousness which constitutes the coming of age of a nation. Tears, as we read in Wordsworth, to human suffering are due; if there be anyone with tears at command he may shed them, with great fitness, and with no profit at all, over the long martyrdom of Ireland. But let him, at least if he values facts, think twice before he goes on to apply to her that other line which speaks of human hopes defeated and overthrown. No other people in the world has held so staunchly to its inner vision; none other has, with such fiery patience, repelled the hostility of circumstances, and in the end reshaped them after the desire of her heart. Hats off to success, gentlemen! Your modern God may well be troubled at sight of this enigmatic Ireland which at once despises him, and tumbles his faithfullest worshippers in the sand of their own amphitheatre. Yet, so it is. The Confederate General, seeing victory suddenly snatched from his hands, and not for the first time, by Meagher's Brigade, exclaimed in immortal profanity: 'There comes that damned Green Flag again!' I have often commended that phrase to Englishmen as admirably expressive of the historical rôle and record of Ireland in British Politics. The damned Green Flag flutters again in their eyes, and if they will but listen to the music that marches with it, they will find that the lamenting fifes are dominated wholly by the drums of victory.

CHAPTER IV

The Obviousness of Home Rule

Ireland, then, has made it her foible to be not only right but irresistible in her past demands. What is it that she now claims, and on what grounds? She claims the right to enter into possession of her own soul. She claims the *toga virilis*, and all the strengthening burdens of freedom. Now it is difficult to represent such a demand in terms of argument. Liberty is no mere conclusion of linked logic long-drawn out: it is an axiom, a flaming avatar. The arguments by which it is defended are important, but they bear to it much the same relation that a table of the wave-lengths of various rays of light bears to the immediate glory of a sunrise. There is another obstacle. Self-government, like other spiritual realities, say love or civilisation, is too vast, obvious, and natural to be easily imprisoned in words. You are certainly in love; suppose you were suddenly asked 'to state the case' for love? You are probably civilised; suppose you were suddenly asked 'to state the case for civilisation'? So it is with the Home Rule idea. To ask what is the gate of entrance to it is like asking what was the gate of entrance to hundred-gated Thebes. My friend, Mr Barry O'Brien, in lecturing on Ireland, used to begin by recounting a very agreeable and appropriate story. A prisoner on trial was asked whether he would accept for his case the jury which had tried the last. He objected very vehemently.

'Well, but', said the Judge, 'what is the nature of your objection? Do you object to the panel or to the array?' 'Ah!' replied the traverser, 'if you want to know, I object to the whole damned business.' That is approximately our objection to the present system of government in Ireland. But let me attempt to group under a series of somewhat arbitrary headings the 'case for Home Rule', that is to say, the case for applying to Ireland the plain platitudes of constitutional freedom.

The whole matter roots in the fact of nationality. Nationality is to political life what personality is to mental life, the mainspring, namely, of the mechanism. The two principles of organisation have this in common, that although by, through, and for them the entire pageant of our experience is unfolded, we are unable to capture either of them in a precise formula. That I am a person I know; but what is a person? That Ireland is a nation I know; but what is a nation? 'A community of memories and hopes', says Anatole France; but that applies to a football club. Something for which a man will die, says Mr T. M. Healy: but men will die for strange reasons; there was a French poet who shot himself because the trees were always green in the spring and never, for a change, blue or red. A cultural unit, say the anthropologists; an idea of the divine mind, declare Mazzini and the mystics of sociology. Each of these formulæ possesses a certain relative truth, but all of them together come short of the whole truth. Nationality, which acts better perhaps than it argues, is one of the great forces of nature and of human nature that have got to be accepted. Nationality will out, and where it exists it will, in spite of all resistance, strain fiercely to express itself in some sort of autonomous government.

German romance depicts for us the misery and restlessness of a man who had lost his shadow. Catholic theologians – if the masters of a wisdom too high and too austere for these days may be invoked – tell us that the departed soul, even though it be in Paradise, hungers with a great desire for the Resurrection that it may be restored to its life-long comrade, the body.

> The crimson-throbbing glow
> Into its old abode aye pants to go.[10]

Look again at Ireland and you will discern, under all conflicts, that unity of memory, of will, of material interest, of temperamental atmosphere which knits men into a nation. You will notice the presence of these characteristics, but it is an absence, a void that will most impress you. You will see not a body that has lost its shadow, but something more sinister – a soul that has been sundered from its natural body. She demands restoration. She sues out a *habeas corpus* of a kind not elsewhere to be paralleled. That is the 'Irish Question'.

You may not like this interpretation of things. It may seem to you fantastic, nasty, perilous to all comfort. Life often does make on the tender-hearted an impression of coarse violence; life, nevertheless, always has its way. What other interpretation is possible? Lancashire, to take any random contrast, is much richer than Ireland in wealth and population; but Lancashire is not a 'Question'. Lancashire is not a 'Question' because Lancashire is not a nation. Ireland is a 'Question' because Ireland is a nation. Her fundamental claim is a claim for the constitutional recognition of nationality.

We have seen that in almost every conflict between English and Irish ideas the latter have had the justification of success. This holds good also as regards our long insistence on nationality as a principle of political organisation. In various passages of the nineteenth century it seemed to be gravely compromised. Capital, its mobility indefinitely increased by the improved technique of exchange, became essentially a citizen of the world. The earth was all about it where to choose; its masters, falsely identifying patriotism with the Protectionism then dominant, struck at both, and the Free Trade movement philosophised itself into cosmopolitanism. Labour, like capital, showed a rapid tendency to become international or rather supernational. 'The workers', proclaimed Marx, 'have no fatherland'. While this was the drift of ideas in the economic sphere, that in the political was no more favourable. Belgium seemed on the point of extinction, Italy was a mere geographical expression, Hungary was abject and broken. In the narrower but even more significant sphere of British colonial policy the passion for centralisation had not yet been understood in all its folly. Downing Street still functioned as the Dublin Castle of the Empire. The possibility of the overseas possessions developing that rich, strong individuality which characterises them to-day would have been dismissed with horror. The colour and texture of men's thought on these subjects has undergone a notable transformation. Cosmopolitanism of the old type is a slain hallucination. Capital in our time is not content to be a patriot, it is a Jingo. As to labour, if we turn to its politics we find Herr Bebel declaring that the German socialist is first of all a German, and Mr Ramsay MacDonald pledging his adherents to support any war necessary for the assertion of English prestige. If we turn to its theoretical sociology we find the national idea rehabilitated and triumphant.

Such intellectual reconstructions do not, as a rule, begin in England, or find in English their characteristic formulæ. Mr Blatchford might indeed be cited, but it is in the brilliant literature of German Social Democracy that the most scientific expression of the new spirit is to be sought. Truly Marx has been indeed translated. His abstract and etiolated internationalism has been replaced by the warm humanity of writers like, say, David or Pernerstorfer. The principle of nationality is vindicated by the latter in a noble passage. I quote it from Sombart's *Socialism and the Social Movement*.[11]

Nationality in its highest form is . . . a precious possession. It is the highest expression of human civilisation in an individual form, and mankind is the richer for its appearance. Our purpose is not only to see to it that men shall be housed and fed and clothed in a manner worthy of human beings, but also that they may become humanised by participation in the culture of centuries, that they may themselves possess culture and produce it. All culture is national. It takes its rise in some special people, and reaches its highest form in national character. . . . Socialism and the national idea are thus not opposed to each other. Every attempt to weaken the national idea is an attempt to lessen the precious possessions of mankind. . . . Socialism wants to organise, and not disintegrate, humanity. But in the organisms of mankind, not individuals, but nations are the tissues, and if the whole organism is to remain healthy it is necessary for the tissues to be healthy. . . . The peoples, despite the changes they undergo, are everlasting, and they add to their own greatness by helping the world upward. And so we are at one and the same time good Socialists and good Germans.

This might almost seem to be a rhapsody, but every movement of continental politics in recent times confirms and enforces its plain truth. 'The spirit of resurgent nationality', as Professor Bury of Cambridge tells us, 'has governed, as one of the most puissant forces, the political course of the last century and is still unexhausted.' It has governed not only the West but the East; the twain have met in that demand for a constitutional national State which in our day has flamed up, a fire not to be put out, in Turkey, Persia, Egypt. But it is in Imperial politics that the bouleversement has been most complete. When critics now find fault with the struture of the Empire they complain not that there is too much Downing Street in it, but that the residual power of Downing Street is not visible to the naked eye. To us Irish the blindness of England to the meaning of her own colonial work is a maddening miracle. A wit of the time met Goldsmith at dinner. The novelist was a little more disconcerting than usual, a result, let us charitably hope, of the excellence of the claret. Afterwards they asked his fellow-diner what he thought of the author. 'Well', he replied, 'I believe that that man wrote *The Vicar of Wakefield*, and, let me tell you, it takes a lot of believing.' Similarly when we in Ireland learn that Great Britain has founded on the principle of local autonomy an Empire on which the sun never sets, we nerve ourselves to an Act of Faith. It is not inappropriate to observe that a large part of the 'founding' was done by Irishmen.

But the point of immediate interest lies in this. The foolishness of England in Ireland finds an exact parallel, although on a smaller scale and for a shorter period, in the early foolishness of England in her own colonies. In both cases there is an attempt to suppress individuality and initiative, to exploit, to bully, to Downing Street-ify. It was a policy of Unionism, the sort of Unionism that linked the destiny of the lady to that of the tiger. The fruits of it were a little bitter in the eating. The colonies in which under the Home Rule regime 'loyalty' has blossomed like the rose, were in those days most distressingly disloyal.

Cattle-driving and all manner of iniquities of that order in Canada; the boycott adopted not as a class, but as a national, weapon in Cape Colony; the Eureka stockade in Australia; Christian De Wet and the crack of Mausers in the Transvaal – such were the propædeutics to the establishment of freedom and the dawn of loyalty in the overseas possessions. But in this field of government the gods gave England not only a great pioneer, Lord Durham, but also the grace to listen to him. His Canadian policy set a headline which has been faithfully and fruitfully copied. Its success was irresistible. Let the *Cambridge Modern History* tell the tale of before and after Home Rule in the Dominion:

Provincial jealousies have dwindled to vanishing point; racial antipathies no longer imperil the prosperity of the Dominion; religious animosities have lost their mischievous power in a new atmosphere of common justice and toleration. Canada, as the direct outcome of Confederation, has grown strong, prosperous, energetic. The unhappy divisions which prevailed at the beginning of the nineteenth century, and which darkened with actual revolt and bloodshed the dawn of the Victorian era, are now only a memory. The links which bind the Dominion to Great Britain may on paper seem slight, but they are resistless. Imperial Federation has still great tasks to accomplish within our widely scattered Imperial domains, but its success in Canada may be accepted as the pledge of its triumph elsewhere. Canada is a nation within the Empire, and in Kipling's phrase is 'daughter in her mother's house and mistress in her own'.

This is the authentic harvest of freedom.

The 'unity' of the old regime which, in a Bismarckian phrase, was like paper pasted over ever-widening cracks, was abandoned. The Separatist programme triumphed. And the outcome? The sham unity of government has been replaced by a real unity of interest, affection and cultural affinity. We find administrators like Mr Lyttleton, former Tory Secretary for the Colonies, engaged to-day not in suppressing but in celebrating the 'varied individuality' of the overseas possessions. As for the political effects of the change, every English writer repeats of the Colonies what Grattan, in other circumstances, said of the Irish: Loyalty is their foible. There is indeed one notable flaw in the colonial parallel. I have spoken as if the claim of the Colonies on foot of the principle of nationality was comparable to that of Ireland. That of course was not the case. They were at most nations in the making; she was a nation made. Home Rule helped on their growth; in its benign warmth Australia, Canada, New Zealand, and South Africa have developed not only a political complexion characteristic of each but a literature, an art and even a slang equally characteristic. Ireland, on the other hand, has manifested throughout her whole history an amazing faculty of assimilating and nationalising everything that came to her from without.

The will to preserve her nationality motived her whole life, especially in the modern period. The declared dream of Grattan was, as we have seen, to transform a Protestant colony into an Irish nation. Wolfe Tone confessed the same inspiration; Emmet's speech from the dock was that and nothing else. It was the whole of Davis in thought, and of O'Connell in action. Isaac Butt yielded to its fascination, and found for it the watchword, Home Rule. It was formulated by Parnell in a speech the capital passage of which forms the inscription on his monument. It echoes and re-echoes through the resolutions of every meeting, and constitutes for many orators their total stock of political ideas. It provides the title of the Irish delegation to Parliament, and is endorsed at General Election after General Election by a great and unchanging majority. A people such as this is not to be exterminated. An ideal such as this is not to be destroyed. Recognise the one, sever the ligatures that check the free flow of blood through the veins of the other, and enrich your federation of autonomous peoples with another rich individuality. Imitate in Ireland your own wisdom in dealing with the Colonies, and the same policy will bear the same harvest. For justice given the Colonies gave you friendship, as for injustice stubbornly upheld they had given you hatred. The analogy with Ireland is complete so far as the cards have been played. The same human elements are there, the same pride, the same anger, the same willingness to forget anger. Why should the augury fail?

I can hear in imagination the sniff of the unimaginative reader; I can figure to myself his instant dismissal of all these considerations as 'sentiment'. Let the word stand, coloured though it is with associations that degrade it. But is 'sentiment' to be ignored in the fixing of constitutions? Ruskin asks a pertinent question. What is it after all but 'sentiment', he inquires, that prevents a man from killing his grandmother in time of hunger? Sentiment is the most respectable thing in human psychology. No one believes in it more thoroughly than your reactionary Tory. But he wears his heart on his sleeve with a difference. He is so greedily patriotic that he would keep all the patriotism in the world to himself. That he should love his country is natural and noble, a theme so high as to be worthy of Mr Kipling or even Mr Alfred Austin himself. That we should love ours is a sort of middle term between treason and insanity. It is as if a lover were to insist that no poems should be written to any woman except *his* mistress. It is as if he were to put the Coercion Act in force against anyone found shedding tears over the sufferings of any mother except *his* mother. In fact it is the sort of domineering thick-headedness that never fails to produce disloyalty.

The national idea, then, is the foundation of the 'case for Home Rule'. It might indeed be styled the whole case, but this anthem of nationality may be transposed into many keys. Translated into terms of ethics it becomes that noble epigram of Sir Henry Campbell Bannerman's for which I would exchange a whole library of Gladstonian eloquence: 'Good government is no substitute for self-government'. In Ireland we have enjoyed neither. Political subjection has mildewed our destiny, leaf and stem. But were it not so, had we increased in wealth like Egypt, in population like Poland, the vital argument for autonomy would be neither weaker nor stronger. Rich or poor, a man must be master of his own fate. Poor or rich, a nation must be captain of her own soul. In the suburban road in which you live there are probably at least a hundred other households. Now if you were all, each suppressing his individuality, to club together you could build in place of the brick-boxes in which you live a magnificent phalanstery. There you could have more air for your lungs and more art for your soul, a spacious and a gracious life, cheaper washing, cheaper food, and a royal kitchen. But you will not do it. Why? Because it profiteth a man nothing to gain the services of a Paris *maître d'hôtel* and to lose his own soul. In an attic fourteen feet by seven, which he can call his own, a man has room to breathe; in a Renaissance palace, controlled by a committee on which he is in a permanent minority of one, he has no room to breathe. Home Rulers are fond of phrasing their programme as a demand on the part of Ireland that she shall control the management of her domestic affairs. The language fits the facts like a glove. The difference between Unionism and Home Rule is the difference between being compelled to live in an ostentatious and lonely hotel and being permitted to live in a simple, friendly house of one's own.

Translated into terms of administration the gospel of autonomy becomes the doctrine of 'the man on the spot'. That is the Eleven Rule of Imperial Policy, and although it has sometimes been ridden to death, in fact to murder, as in the Denshawai hangings, it is a sound rule. A man who has gone to the trouble of being born, bred, and ordinarily domiciled in, say, Kamskatcka is more likely to understand the affairs of Kamskatcka than a man whose life oscillates daily like a pendulum between Clapham and the Strand. The old natural philosophers accepted the theory of *actio distans*, that is to say they assumed that a body could act effectively where it was not. This was Unionism in science, and needless to say it was wrong. In politics it is equally wrong, and it has been repudiated everywhere except in Ireland. Physical vision is limited in range; as the distance increases the vision declines in clearness, becomes subject to illusion, finally ceases. Now you in London, through mere limitations of human faculty, cannot see us in Dublin. You are trying to govern Ireland in the fashion in which, according to Wordsworth, all bad literature has been written, that is to say, without your eye on the object. But it is time to have done with this stern, long chase of the obvious.

Translated into terms of economics the gospel of autonomy becomes the doctrine of a 'stake in the country'. England has, indeed, a stake in Ireland. She has the same interest in seeing Ireland prosperous that a bootmaker has in learning from his farmer client that the crops are good. Each country is in great measure the economic complement of the other. But if the bootmaker were to insist on having his finger in the farmer's pie, the pie, destined for the bootmaker's own appetite, would not be improved. If he were to insist on applying to the living cow those processes which he applies with such success to the dead leather, the cow would suffer and ultimately there would be no boots. Generally speaking, each of us improves his own business by declining to mind anybody else's. Home Rule will give England precisely this chance of sticking to her last. To Ireland it will come with both hands full of new opportunities and new responsibilities.

To realise that the national idea in Ireland arouses an emotion, at once massive, intense, and enduring, is to understand many derivative riddles. We are all familiar with the complaint that there is in Ireland too much politics and too little business. Of course there is, and not only too little business but too little literature, too little philosophy, too little social effort, too little fun. We Nationalists have grasped this better and proclaimed it more steadily than any Unionist. There is as much truth in saying that life begins where politics end, as in saying that love begins where love-making ends. Constitutional freedom is not the fifth act of the social drama in modern times, it is rather the prologue, or, better still, the theatre in which other ideas that move men find an arena for their conflict. Ireland, a little exhausted by her intense efforts of the last thirty years, does assuredly need a rest-cure from agitation. But this healing peace is itself a gift of autonomy. A tooth-ache concentrates the whole mind on one particular emotion, which is a bad thing, and breeds profanity, which is worse. But it is idle to tell a man with a tooth-ache that what he needs in his life is less cursing and more business. He cannot work effectively so long as he suffers; the only way to peace is to cure the tooth-ache. And in order to get rid of politics in Ireland, you must give Ireland Home Rule.

CHAPTER V

The Ravages of Unionism (1)

Ireland, as we have seen, has had the misfortune to provoke many worthy writers to a sad debauch of sentimentalism. It has pleased their fancy especially to picture her as a sphinx, mysterious, elusive, inscrutable. It is impossible to govern her, declare these theorists, because it is impossible to understand her. She is the *femme incomprise* of modern politics. Her temperament is a magnet for disaster, her soul a sanctuary of inviolable secrets. So runs the rhapsody, and many of my own countrymen have thought it good strategy to accept and exploit it. They have this to urge, indeed, that failure to make oneself understood is commonly regarded as a sign of the superior mind. Lord Rosebery, for example, has told us that he himself, for all his honey-dropping tongue, has never been properly understood. And Hegel, the great German philosopher, who was so great a philosopher that we may without impropriety mention his name even in the brilliant vicinage of the Earl of Midlothian, used to sigh: 'Alas! in the whole of my teaching career I had but one student who understood my system, and he mis-understood it.' This is all very well in its way, and a climate of incomprehension may suit orators and metaphysicians admirably; but it will not do for politics. The party or people that fails to make its programme understood is politically incompetent, and Ireland is assuredly safe from any such imputation. She has her spiritual secrets, buried deep in what we may call the subliminal consciousness of the race, and to the disclosure of these secrets we may look with confidence for the inspiration of a new literature. But in politics Ireland has no secrets. All her cards are on the table, decipherable at the first glance. Her political demand combines the lucidity of an invoice with the axiomatic rectitude of the Ten Commandments. There is no doubt about what she wants, and none about why she ought to have it. In that sense the case for Home Rule is made, and this book, having justified its title, ought to come to an end. But convention prescribes that about the nude contour of principles there should be cast a certain drapery of details, and such conventions are better obeyed.

Where we are to begin is another matter. We are, as has been so often suggested, in presence of a situation in which one cannot see the trees for the forest. The principle of the government of Ireland is so integrally wrong that it is difficult to signalise any one point in which it is more wrong than it is in any other. A timber-chaser, that is to say a pioneer for a lumber firm, in the Western States of America once found himself out of spirits. He decided to go out of life, and being thorough in his ways he left nothing to chance. He set fire to his cabin, and, mounting the table, noosed his neck to a beam, drank a large quantity of poison, and, as he kicked over the table, simultaneously shot himself through the head and drew a razor across his throat. Later on the doctor had to fill in the usual certificate. At 'Cause of Death' he paused, pondered, and at last wrote, 'Causes too numerous to specify.' The fable possesses a certain suggestive value upon which we need not enlarge. How, one may well ask, are we to itemise the retail iniquities of a system of government which is itself a wholesale iniquity? But since we must begin somewhere let us begin with the Economics of Unionism.

In this often-written, and perhaps over-written story there is one feature of some little comfort. Whatever quarrel there may be as to causes, the facts are not disputed. Pitt and his friends promised that the Union would be followed by general prosperity, development of manufacturers, and expansion of commerce.

'Among the great and known defects of Ireland', he declared in a typical statement, 'one of the most prominent features is its want of industry and of capital. How are these wants to be supplied but by blending more closely with Ireland the industry and capital of Great Britain?'

It was a Witches' Promise making smooth the path to damnation. In every point in which Pitt had prophesied white the moving finger of history began, from the very day of the Union, to write black. The injury to the whole economic tissue of Ireland was immediate, cumulative, in the end crushing.

We have at hand authoritative figures of the decline collected by various Commissions and private inquirers. Let us note some of these as summarised by Monsignor O'Riordan in his remarkable book, *Catholicism and Progress*:[12]

Again, in 1800 there were 91 woollen manufacturers in Dublin and 4,938 hands employed; in 1840 there were only 12 manufacturers, and 682 hands employed; in 1880, only 3 manufacturers in Dublin and around it. In 1800 there were 56 blanket manufacturers in Kilkenny, and 3,000 hands employed; in 1840 there were 12 manufacturers and 925 hands employed. In 1800 there were 900 hands employed on ratteens and friezes in Roscrea; in 1840 the industry had completely disappeared. In 1800 there were 1,000 flannel looms in County Wicklow; in 1840 there was not one. In 1800 there were 2,500 looms at work in Dublin for the manufacture of silk and poplin; in 1840 there were only 250. In 1800 there were 27,000 cotton workers in Belfast and around it; in 1840 there were only 12,000. In 1800 there were 61,075 tradesmen in Dublin for the woollen, silk, and cotton industries; in 1834 there were only 14,446, and of these 4,412 were idle, showing a decrease of 51,041 in the employed.

There was, we must add, an increase in other directions. For instance, whereas there had been only seven bankruptcies decreed in Dublin in 1799 there were 125 in 1810. The number of insolvent houses grew in seven years from 880 to 4,719. These figures are not random but symptomatic. Mr Pitt had promised to blend Ireland with the capital and industry of Great Britain; he blended them as the edge of a tomahawk is blended with the spattered brains of its victim. We have glanced at the condition of manufacture. Lest it should be assumed that the tiller of land at least had profited by the Napoleonic Wars, with their consequent high prices, let me hasten to add that the Grey Commission, reporting in 1836, had to inform the Government that 2,385,000 persons, nearly one-third of the population, were 'in great need of food'.

'Their habitations', the Report proceeds, 'are wretched hovels; several of the family sleep together on straw, or on the bare ground, sometimes with a blanket, sometimes not even so much to cover them. Their food commonly consists of dry potatoes; and with these they are at times so scantily supplied as to be obliged to stint themselves to one spare meal in the day. . . . They sometimes get a herring or a little milk, but they never get meat except at Christmas, Easter, and Shrovetide.'

But a truce to these dismal chronicles. The *post hoc* may be taken as established; was it a *propter hoc*? Was the Union the cause as well as the antecedent of this decay? No economist, acquainted with the facts, can fail to answer in the affirmative. The causal connection between two realities could not be more manifest. Let us examine it very briefly.

I begin of necessity with the principle of freedom, for freedom is the dominating force in economic life. No instance can be cited of a modern people of European civilisation that ever prospered while held politically in subjection.

'All history', writes Professor Marshall of Cambridge, the doyen of Political Economy in England, 'is full of the record of inefficiency caused in varying degrees by slavery, serfdom, and other forms of civil and political oppression and repression.'[13]

The Act of Union was, as has been said, one of those spiritual outrages which, in their reactions, are like lead poured into the veins. It lowered the vital resources of Ireland. It made hope an absentee, and enterprise an exile. That was its first-fruits of disaster.

These commonplaces of the gospel of freedom 'for which Hampden died in the field and Sidney on the scaffold' will possibly appear to their modern descendants mystical, sentimental, and remote from real life. For there is no one in the world so ready as your modern Englishman to deny that he is a man in order to prove that he is a business-man. Fortunately we can establish for this strange being, who has thus indecently stripped himself of humanity, and establish in very clear and indisputable fashion the cash nexus between Unionism and decay. The argument is simple.

The Union came precisely in the period in which capital was beginning to dominate the organisation of industry. The Union denuded Ireland of the capital which would have enabled her to transform the technique of her manufactures, and so maintain the ground won under Grattan's Parliament. The channels through which this export of capital proceeded were absenteeism and over-taxation.

The first statement in this paragraph of plaint calls for no elaboration. Arnold Toynbee took as the terminal dates of the Industrial Revolution the years 1760 and 1830. The last generation of the eighteenth century brought to birth the great inventions, but it was the first generation of the nineteenth that founded on them large scale production, and settled the structure of modern industry. Not without profound disturbance and incalculable suffering was the new system established in England; the story may be read in the pages of Marx, Cunningham, Cooke Taylor, or any of the economic historians. But, for all the blood and tears, it was established. Insulated from the continental turmoil, served by her Titanic bondsmen coal and iron, England was able to defeat the Titan, Napoleon. Now it is idle to deny that this period would under any government have strained Ireland, as the phrase goes, to the pin of her collar. But the Union made her task impossible. Lord Castlereagh was quite right in pointing to the accumulation of capital as the charactcristic advantage of England. Through centuries of political freedom that process had gone on without interruption. Ireland, on the contrary, had been scientifically pillaged by the application to her of the 'colonial system' from 1663 to 1779; I deliberately exclude the previous waste of war and confiscation. She had but twenty years of commercial freedom, and, despite her brilliant success in that period, she had not time to accumulate capital to any great extent. But Grattan's Parliament had shown itself extraordinarily astute and steady of purpose in its economic policy. Had its guidance continued – conservative taxation, adroit bounties, and that close scrutiny and eager discussion of the movements of industry which stands recorded in its Journal the manufactures of Ireland would have weathered the storm. But the luck was as usual against her. Instead of wise leadership from Dublin the gods decreed that she should have for portion the hard indifference and savage taxation of Westminster. Reduced to the position of a tributary nation, stripped of the capital that would have served as a commissariat of advance in that crucial struggle, she went down.

I am not to make here the case for Ireland in respect of over-taxation. It was made definitely in the Report of the Childers Commission, a document which no Englishman reads, lest in

coming to the light he should have his sins too sharply rebuked. It
has been developed and clarified in many speeches and essays and
in some books. To grasp it is to find your road to Damascus on the
Irish Question. But for the moment we are concerned with but one
aspect, namely, the export of capital from Ireland as a result of the
Union, and the economic reactions of that process. Since we are to
use moderation of speech and banish all rhetoric from these pages,
one is at a loss to characterise Union arrangements and post-
Union finance. Let it suffice to say that they combined the moral
outlook of Captain Kidd with the mathematical technique of a
super-bucket-shop. From the first Great Britain robbed the Irish
till; from the first she skimmed the cream off the Irish milk, and
appropriated it for her own nourishment. One has a sort of gloomy
pride in remembering that although cheated in all these trans-
actions we were not duped. Mr Foster, Speaker of the Irish House
of Commons – in those days the Speaker actually spoke, a whimsical
Irish custom – tore the cloak off Lord Castlereagh's strutting
statesmanship, and laid bare his real motives. Speaking on the first
Union proposal in 1799 he said:

> But the noble Lord has told us the real motives of this scheme of
> Union, and I thank him for stating them so fairly. Ireland, he says,
> must contribute to every war, and the Minister won't trust to interest,
> affection, or connection for guiding her conduct. *He must have her
> purse within his own grasp.* While three hundred men hold it in Ireland
> he cannot put his hand into it, they are out of his reach, but let a
> hundred of you carry it over and lay it at his feet, and then he will have
> full and uncontrolled power.

So it came about. Even before the Union Grattan's Parliament
had, of its own free will and out of an extravagant loyalty, run itself
into debt for the first time to help England against France. But, as

Foster indicated, the Irish members felt that they were coming to the end of their resources. They were about to call a halt, and so the Union became a necessary ingredient of Pitt's foreign policy. By it Ireland was swept into the vortex of his anti-French hysteria, and of what Mr Hartley Withers so properly styles his 'reckless finance'. In sixteen years she was brought to the edge of bankruptcy. Between 1801 and 1817 her funded debt was increased from £28,541,157 to £112,684,773, an augmentation of nearly 300 per cent. In the first fifteen years following the Union she paid in taxes £78,000,000 as against £31,000,000 in the last fifteen years preceding the Union. After the amalgamation of the Exchequers in 1817 the case becomes clearer. In 1819–20, for instance, the revenue contributed by Ireland was £5,256,564, of which only £1,564,880 was spent in Ireland, leaving a tribute for Great Britain of £3,691,684. For 1829–30 the tribute was £4,156,576.

Let us now inquire how things stood with regard to absenteeism. This had existed before the Union; indeed, if the curious reader will turn to Johnson's 'Dictionary' he will find it damned in a definition. But it was enormously intensified by the shifting of the centre of gravity of Irish politics, industry, and fashion from Dublin to London. The memoirs of that day abound in references to an exodus which has left other and more material evidence in those fallen and ravaged mansions which now constitute the worst slums of our capital city.

One figure may be cited by way of illustration. Before the Union '98 Peers, and a proportionate number of wealthy Commoners' lived in Dublin. The number of resident Peers in 1825 was twelve. At present, as I learn from those who read the sixpenny illustrateds, there is one. But when they abandoned Ireland they did not leave their rents behind. And it was a time of rising rents; according to Toynbee they at least doubled between 1790 and 1833. Precise figures are not easily arrived at, but Mr D'Alton in his

History of the County Dublin,[14] a book quite innocent of politics, calculates that the absentee rental of Ireland was in 1804 not less than £3,000,000, and in 1830 not less than £4,000,000, an underestimate. If we average these figures over the period we find that during the first thirty years of Union, that is to say during the most critical phase of the Industrial Revolution, not less than £105,000,000 of Irish capital was 'exported' from Ireland to Great Britain through the channel of absenteeism.

Averaging the figures of the taxation-tribute in similar fashion, and taking the lowest estimates, I am unable to reach a less total than £120,000,000 for the same period. In other words, the effect of the Union was to withdraw from Ireland during the thirty years that settled the economic structure of modern industry not less than £225,000,000. Let me draw the argument together in words which I have used elsewhere, and which others can no doubt easily better:

> We have heard, in our day, a long-drawn denunciation of a Liberal government on the score that it had, by predatory taxation, driven English capital out of the country, and compromised the industrial future of England. We have seen in our own day gilt-edged securities, bank, insurance, railway, and brewery shares in Great Britain, brought toppling down by a Tory waste of £250,000,000 on the Boer War. We know that in economic history effects are, in a notable way, cumulative; so clearly marked is the line of continuity as to lead a great writer to declare that there is not a nail in all England that could not be traced back to savings made before the Norman Conquest. A hundred instances admonish us that, in industrial life, nothing fails like failure. When we put all these considerations together, and give them a concrete application, can we doubt that in over-taxation and the withdrawal of capital we have the prime *causa causans* of the decay of Ireland under the Union?

In this wise did Pitt 'blend Ireland with the industry and capital of Great Britain'. Cupped by his finance she gave the venal blood of her industry to strengthen the predominant partner, and to help him to exclude for a time from these islands that pernicious French Democracy in which all states and peoples have since found redemption. Such was the first chapter in the Economics of Unionism.

CHAPTER VI

The Ravages of Unionism (2)

If the reader cares to push forward the line of thought suggested in the preceding pages and to submit it to a concrete test he can do so without difficulty. He has but to compare the post-Union history of linen with that of cotton. Linen in Ireland had been a perfect type of the State-created, spoon-fed industry character-istic of the period of mercantilism. Within certain limits – such as the steady resolve to confine it, in point of religion, to Protestants, and, in point of geography, to Ulster – it had behind it at the Union a century of encouragement. It is calculated that between 1700 and 1800 it had received bounties, English and Irish, totalling more than, £2,500,000. In other words it had a chance to accu-mulate capital. Even linen declined after the Union partly from the direct effects of that measure, partly from the growing intensity of the Industrial Revolution. But the capital accumulated, the com-mercial good name established under native government carried the manufacturers through. These were able towards 1830 to introduce the new machinery and the new processes, and to weather the tempest of competition. Cotton, on the other hand, was a very recent arrival. It had developed very rapidly, and in 1800 gave promise of supplanting linen. But the weight of capital told more and more as changes in the technique of transportation and production ushered in our modern world. Lacking the solid reserves of its rival, involved in all the exactions that fall on a tributary nation, the cotton manufacture of Ireland lost ground, lost heart, and disappeared.

But let us resume the parable. If the 'business man' responds to capital, he will certainly not be obtuse to the appeal of coal. In this feeder of industry Ireland was geologically at a disadvantage, and it was promised that the free trade with Great Britain inaugurated by the Union would 'blend' with her the resources of the latter country. Did she obtain free trade in coal? Miss Murray, a Unionist, in her *Commercial Relations between England and Ireland* tells the story in part:

> Coals again had hitherto been exported from Great Britain at a duty of 9*d*. per ton; this duty was to cease but the Irish import duty on coal was to be made perpetual, and that at a time when all coasting duties in England and Scotland had been abolished. Dublin especially would suffer from this arrangement, for the duty there on coals imported was is 1*s*. 8 ⁴/₅*d*. per ton, while that in the rest of Ireland was only 9½ *d*. This was because a local duty of 1*s*. per ton existed in Dublin for the internal improvement of the city; this local duty was blended by the Union arrangements with the general duty on the article, and its perpetual continuance was thus enforced. All this shows how little Irish affairs were understood in England.[15]

But was it a failure of the English intellect or a lapse of the English will? Except through the Platonic intuition which reduces all sin to terms of ignorance I cannot accept the former explanation. What is certain is that there was no lack of contemporary protest. There existed in Dublin in 1828 a Society for the Improvement of Ireland, an active body which included in its membership the Lord Mayor (a high Tory, of course), Lord Cloncurry, and a long list of notable names such as Latouche, Sinclair, Houghton, Leader, Grattan, Smith O'Brien, George Moore, and Daniel O'Connell. In the year mentioned the Society appointed a number of committees to report on the state of Irish agriculture, commerce, and industry. One of these reports is full of information touching the drain of capital from the country, and its consequent decay, as registered by contemporaries; we shall learn from another how things stood with regard to coal. At the time of the Union the Irish Parliament granted a bounty of 2s. per ton on Irish coal carried coastwise to Dublin, and levied a duty of 10½ d. per ton on coal imported from Great Britain. The effect of the Union was to abolish the bounty and double the levy on imports. Writing twenty-eight years later the Committee summarise in a brief passage the disastrous effects of a policy, so foolish and so unjust. The last sentence opens up sombre vistas to any student of economic history:

> Severe, however, as the operation of the coal duty in arresting the progress of manufacture may have been in other parts of Ireland, in Dublin, under the circumstances to which your Committee are about to call the attention of the Society, it has produced all the effects of actual prohibition, all the mischiefs of the most rigorous exclusion. It is a singular circumstance that, in the metropolis of the country, possessing local advantages in respect to manufactures and facilities for trade with the interior, superior, probably, to any other city or town in this portion of the empire, with a population excessive as to the means of employment, in a degree which probably has not a parallel in Europe, *there is not a factory for the production of either silk, linen, cotton, or woollen manufactures which is worked or propelled by a steam engine*.

The writers go on to ask for the repeal of the local duty on coal in Dublin, and to suggest that the necessary revenue should be raised by a duty on spirits. This course Belfast had been permitted to follow – one of the numberless make-weights thrown into the scale so steadily on the side of the Protestant North. In my part of the country the people used to say of any very expert thief: 'Why, he'd steal the fire out of your grate.' Under the Union arrangements Great Britain stole the fire out of the grate of Ireland. And having so dealt with capital and coal the predominant partner next proceeded by a logical development to muddle transportation.

The Drummond Commission, appointed in 1836 to consider the question of railway construction in Ireland, issued a report in 1838 which practically recommended public and not private enterprise as appropriate 'to accomplish so important a national object'. What came after is best related in the official terminology of the Scotter Commission of 1906–10:

> This report was presented in July 1838, and early in the following year a great public meeting, held in Dublin, passed a resolution that inasmuch as an adequate system of railways could not be constructed by private capital, the Government should be urged to take the work into its own hands, thereby saving the cost of Private Bill legislation. Promises were also made that the lands necessary for railway construction would be given free of cost. Similar resolutions were adopted at another meeting held about the same time in the north of Ireland. In addition, an address to the Queen was presented by a number of Irish Peers, headed by the Duke of Leinster, praying that action might be taken on the Drummond Commission Report.

The government saw the light, and proceeded to sin against it. They embodied the Dublin programme in resolutions which were adopted by the House of Commons in March 1839, and they then abruptly abandoned the whole business. The last chance was not yet lost. During the Great Famine of 1847 the Opposition proposed to raise £16,000,000 by State loans for the construction of railways as relief works. A suggestion so sane could not hope to pass. It was in fact rejected; the starving peasants were set to dig large holes and fill them up again, and to build bad roads leading nowhere. And instead of a national railway system Ireland was given private enterprise with all its waste and all its clash of interests.

The two most conspicuous gifts of Unionism to Ireland have been, as all the world knows, poverty and police. Soon after 1830, that is to say when the first harvest of government from Westminster was ripe to the sickle, Irish destitution had assumed what politicians call menacing proportions. One person in every three of the population never had any other alimentary experience than the difference between hunger and starvation. In these circumstances a Royal Commission was appointed to consider the advisability of extending the English Poor Law to Ireland. Their report is a pioneer document in the development of economic thought. Just as the Railway Commission a few years later was to give the watchword of the future, nationalisation, so the Poor Law Commission gave within its province the watchword of the future, prevention before relief. They pointed the contrast between the two countries. I quote the words of the later Irish Poor Law Commission of 1903–6:

Having regard to the destitution and poverty that were prevalent in Ireland owing to want of employment, the Royal Commissioners in their Report of 1836 came to the conclusion that the English work-house system would be unsuitable for Ireland, because after unchecked demoralisation by profuse out-door relief *in England, the Work-house system was devised in order to make the lazy and idle seek ordinary employment which could be got. The situation in Ireland was, on the contrary, one in which the able-bodied and healthy were willing and anxious to work for any wages, even for twopence a day, but were unable to obtain such or any employment.*

Ireland at the end of a generation of Unionism was suffering, as the commissioners proceed to point out, not from over-population, but from under-development. They tabled two sets of recommendations. The relief programme advised compulsory provision for the sick, aged, infirm, lunatics, and others incapable of work; in all essential matters it anticipated in 1836 that Minority Report which to the England of 1912 still seems extravagantly humane. The prevention programme outlined a scheme for the development of Irish resources. Including, as it did, demands for County Fiscal Boards, agricultural education, better cottages for the labourers, drainage, reclamation, and changes in the land system, it has been a sort of lucky bag into which British ministers have been dipping without acknowledgment ever since. But the report itself was, like the Railway Report, too sane and too Irish to stand a chance. There was sent over from England a Mr Nicholls, who, after a six weeks flutter through the country, devised the Poor Law System under which we still labour. Mr Nicholls afterwards became Sir George, and when he died it is probable that a statue was erected to him. If that is so the inscription must always remain inadequate until this is added: 'Having understood all about Ireland in six weeks he gave her, as the one thing needful to redeem her, the workhouse.'

But, of course, the capital exploit of the Economics of Unionism was its dealing with the problem of land tenure. I shrink from inviting the reader into the desert of selfishness and stupidity which constitutes English policy, in this regard, from the Union to the triumph of the Land League. Let him study it at large in Davitt's *Fall of Feudalism*.[16] We are not concerned here to revive that calamitous pageant. Our interest is of another kind, namely to signalise the malign influence introduced into the agrarian struggle by government from Westminster as against government from Dublin. Even had Grattan's Parliament remained, the battle for the land would have had to go forward; for that Parliament was an assembly controlled by landlords who, for the most part, believed as strongly in the sacredness of rent as they did in the sacredness of nationality. But by the Union the conflict was embittered and befouled. The landlords invented their famous doctrine of conditional loyalty. They bargained with Great Britain to the effect that, if they were permitted to pillage their tenantry, they would in return uphold and maintain British rule in Ireland.

It was the old picture with which M. Paul-Dubois has acquainted us, that of the 'Garrison' kneeling to England on the necks of the Irish poor. In this perversion, which under autonomy would have been impossible, we find the explanation of the extreme savagery of Union land policy in Ireland. Its extreme, its bat-eyed obtuseness is to be explained in another way. Souchon in his introduction to the French edition of Philippovich, the great Austrian economist, observes with great truth that England has not even yet developed any sort of *Agrarpolitik*, that is to say any systematic Economics of Agriculture. In the early nineteenth century her own land problems were neglected, and her political leaders were increasingly dominated by an economic gospel of shopkeepers and urban manufacturers. Forced into the context of agrarian life such a gospel was bound to manifest itself as one of folly and disaster.

If we put these two elements together we are enabled to understand why the Union land policy in Ireland was such a portentous muddle and scandal. In 1829 the question assumed a fresh urgency, in consequence of the eviction campaign which followed the disfranchisement of the small holders under Catholic Emancipation. That Irish opinion, which in an Irish Parliament would have had its way, began to grapple with the situation.

Between 1829 and 1858 twenty-three Irish Land Reform Bills were introduced in the House of Commons; every one was rejected. In the same period thirty-five Coercion Bills were introduced; every one was passed. So it began, so it continued, until at last Irish opinion did in some measure prevail. The Westminster Parliament clapped the 'agitators' into prison, and while they were at work breaking stones stole their programme. . . . But I have promised to spare the reader the detailed hideousness of this Inferno, and this section must close without a word said about that miserable triad, famine, eviction, and emigration. What may be called the centre of relevancy lies elsewhere. We have been concerned to show how Unionism, having wrecked the whole manufacturing economy of Ireland, went on, at its worst, to wreck, at its best, to refuse to save, its whole agricultural economy.

But why recall all this 'dead history'? For two reasons: first, because it illustrates the fundamental wrongness of Unionism; secondly, because it is not dead.

On the first point no better authority can be found than Mr W. A. S. Hewins, the intellect of Tariff Reform. The differences between England and Ireland, he writes in his introduction to Miss Murray's book, are of 'an organic character'. In that phrase is concentrated the whole biology of Home Rule. Every organism must suffer and perish unless its external circumstances echo its inner law of development. The sin of the Union was that it imposed on Ireland from without a sort of spiked strait-jacket which could have no effect but to squeeze the blood and breath out of every interest in the country. What was meat to England was poison to Ireland, and even honest Englishmen, hypnotised by the economists of the day, were unable to perceive this plain truth. Let me give another illustration. The capital exploit of Union Economics was, as has been said, its dealing with the land question, but perhaps its most pathetic fallacy was the policy with which it met the Great Famine. Now the singular thing about this famine is that during it there was no scarcity of food in Ireland; there was only a shortage of potatoes.

'In 1847 alone', writes Mr Michael Davitt in his *Fall of Feudalism*, 'food to the value of £44,958,000 sterling was grown in Ireland

according to the statistical returns for that year. But a million of
people died for want of food all the same.'

The explanation is obvious: the peasants grew potatoes to feed
themselves, they raised corn to pay their rents. A temporary sus-
pension of rent-payments and the closing of the ports would have
saved the great body of the people. But the logic of Unionism
worked on other lines. The government opened the ports, cheap-
ened corn, and made rents harder to pay. At the same time they
passed a new Coercion Act, and reorganised the police on its
present basis to ensure that rents should be paid. To the wisdom of
this policy, history is able to call witnesses by the million – unhappily
however it has to call them from famine graveyards, and the waste
womb of the Atlantic.

This essential wrongness of Unionism, so amply illustrated
in every year of its working, continues. But at least, our bluff
Englishman urges, the dead past can be suffered to bury those
crimes and blunders of Unionism which you have enumerated.
Let us start with a clean slate. Now, as will have been gathered
from a previous chapter, we recognise in this invitation an accent
of soundness. We modern Home Rulers desire above all to be loyal
to the century in which we live. We are sick of that caricature
which depicts Ireland as the mad heroine of a sort of perpetual
suttee, in which all the interests of the present are immolated on
the funeral-pyre of the past. But let us come closer to things. How
do you clean a slate except by liquidating the debts of which it
keeps the record? The late Vicomte de Voguë wrote an admirable
novel, *Les Morts qui parlent*.[17] The dead are always speaking; you
cannot stop their strong eloquence with a mouthful of clay. The
'business man' thinks no doubt that the Napoleonic War is no more
than Hecuba to him, or he to Hecuba. But he pays annual tribute
to it, for he has to make annual provision for the £600,000,000
which it added to the National Debt. And just as Mr Pitt's foreign

policy is in that respect a living reality of our own time, so also, but in a much graver form, are the past depredations and ineptitudes of Unionism living realities in the present economy of Ireland.

The ruling fallacy of the English mind on these matters consists in the assumption that the mere repeal of an old oppression restores a people to the *status quo ante*. In the case of Ireland the old oppressions have not been repealed except in two or three points, but even if they had been wholly cancelled it would be absurd to expect immediate recovery from their effects. If you have been beating a man on the head with a bludgeon for half an hour, and then leave off, there is no sense in saying to him: 'There, I have given over bludgeoning you. Why on earth don't you get up, and skip about like me?' If you have been robbing a man's till for ten years, and then decide – by the way you have not yet decided – to leave off, there is no sense in saying to him: 'Why the devil are you always hard up? Look at me doing the same sort of business as you on absolutely equal terms, and I'm able to keep two motor-cars and six servants.' But that is precisely what is said to us. You are eternally expecting from Ireland new miracles of renaissance. But although she does possess recuperative powers, hardly to be paralleled, even she must have time to slough the corruptions of the past. You cannot, as some Englishmen imagine, cancel six centuries before breakfast. Your Penal Laws, for instance, have been long since struck out of the Statute Book, but they have not yet been eliminated from social habitudes or from certain areas of commercial life.

You began to tax Ireland beyond her capacity in 1801, and you are still overtaxing her. In the interval you withdraw from her economic life a tribute of not less than £325,000,000. You broke her industrial tradition, injured her credit, depressed her confidence. You forced upon her a fiscal system devised to suit your needs in utter contempt of hers. To clean that slate you must first, by some measure of restitution, clean your conscience. And when that has been done you will have to wait for the curative effects of time to undo the Economics of Unionism.

You suffered landlordism to devastate Ireland unchecked. The capital that should have gone to enrich and develop the soil was squeezed out of it in rack-rents, largely absentee. The whole agricultural economy of the country was stricken with a sort of artificial anæmia. Then very late in the day you enact in shreds and fragments a programme of reform proposed half a century before by the leaders of the Irish people. To-day rural Ireland is convalescent, but it is absurd to rate her if she does not at once manifest all the activities of robust health. It is even more absurd to expect her to glow with gratitude.

You muddled our whole system of transportation; your muddle stands to-day in all its ruinous largeness unamended, and, it may be, beyond amendment. You muddled the Poor Law; and, in the workhouses which you thrust upon us, 8,000 children are year by year receiving on their lives the brand of degradation. You marred education, perverting it into a discipline of denationalisation, and that virus has not yet been expelled.

What economic, what intellectual problem in Ireland have you not marred and muddled, England, my England (as the late Mr W. E. Henley used to say)? You have worsened the maledictions of the Bible. The sins of *your* fathers will lie as a *damnosa hæreditas*, a damnable heritage, upon the mortgaged shoulders of our children. It is better, as Plato taught, to suffer injustice than to inflict it. In the light of that ethical principle you are long since judged and condemned. But with the customary luck of England you are allowed what others were not allowed, the opportunity of penitence and reform. The messengers of the new gospel are at your doors, offering you in return for the plain rudiments of justice not only forgiveness but friendship. It is for you to accept or reject. We, the

Irish, whom you have wronged, look to your decision with interest rather than with concern. Why should we be concerned? Our flag has been an Aaron's serpent to swallow yours. Your policies, your ambitions, your administrations have passed by us like the transient and embarrassed phantoms that they were. We remain. All the roads lead to Rome, and all the years to retribution. This is your year; you have met the messengers on your threshold. Your soul is in your own wardship. But yet we cannot wholly separate your destiny from ours. Dedicated as we are to the general progress of humanity and to all the generosities of life, we await expectantly your election between the good and the evil side.

CHAPTER VII

The Hallucination of 'Ulster'

Ulster Unionism, in the leaders, is not so much a programme of ideas as a demand for domination. In the rank and file it is largely a phenomenon of hysteria. I do not know whether my readers have ever participated in an agreeable game known as odd man out. Each player tosses a penny, and whoever disagrees with the rest, showing a head to their tails or vice versa, captures the pool. Such is in all essential particulars the 'Ulster Question'. We find ourselves there in presence of a minority which, on the sole ground that it is a minority, claims that in the government of Ireland it shall be not merely secure but supreme. Sir Edward Carson as odd man out (and I do not deny that he is odd enough for anything) is to be Dictator of Ireland. If eighty-four Irish constituencies declare for Home Rule, and nineteen against Home Rule, then, according to the mathematics of Unionism, the Noes have it. In their non-Euclidean geometry the part is always greater than the whole. In their unnatural history the tail always wags the dog. On the plane of politics it is not necessary to press the case against 'Ulster' any farther than that. Even majorities have their rights. If a plurality of nine to two is not sufficient to determine policy and conduct business in a modern nation, then there is no other choice except anarchy, or rather an insane atomism. Not merely every party, but every household and, in last resort, every individual will end as a Provisional Government. Separatism of this type is a very ecstasy of nonsense, and none of my readers will think so cheaply of his own intelligence as to stay to discuss it. It is in other terms that we must handle the problem of 'Ulster'.

The existence in certain nooks and corners of Ireland of a democratic vote hostile to Home Rule is, let us confess, a conundrum. But it is a conundrum of psychology rather than of politics. It may seem rude to say so, but Orangeism consists mainly of a settled hallucination and an annual brainstorm. No one who has not been present at a 'Twelfth of July procession can realise how completely all its manifestations belong to the life of hysteria and not to that of reason. M. Paul-Dubois, whom we may summon out of a cloud of witnesses, writes of them as 'demagogic orgies with a mixed inspiration of Freemasonry and the Salvation Army'. The Twelfth of July is, or rather was, for its fine furies are now much abated, a savage carnival comparable only to the corroborees of certain primitive tribes.

'A monster procession', continues M. Paul-Dubois, 'marches through Belfast, as through every town and village of Orange Ulster, ending up with a vast meeting at which the glories of William of Orange and the reverses of James II are celebrated in song. . . . Each "lodge" sends its delegation to the procession with banners and drums. On the flags are various devices: "Diamond Heroes", "True Blues", "No Pope". The participants give themselves over to character dances, shouting out their favourite songs: "The Boyne Water" and "Croppies Lie Down". The chief part is played by the drummers, the giants of each "lodge", who with bared arms beat their drums with holy fury, their fists running with blood, until the first drum breaks and many more after it, until in the evening they fall half-dead in an excess of frenzy.'

Such is the laboratory in which the mind of Orange Ulster is prepared to face the tasks of the twentieth century. Barbaric music, the ordinary allowance of drum to fife being three to one, ritual dances, King William on his white horse, the Scarlet Woman on her seven hills, a grand parade of dead ideas and irrelevant ghosts called up in wild speeches by clergymen and politicians – such is Orangeism in its full heat of action. Can we, with this key to its intellectual history, be really astonished that Shankhill Road should move all its life in a red mist of superstition. The North of Ireland abounds in instances, trivial and tragic, of this obsession. Here it is the case of the women of a certain town who, in order to prevent their children from playing in a dangerous swamp close by, have taught them that there are 'wee Popes' in it. There it is a case of man picked up, maimed and all but unconscious after an accident, screwing up his lips to utter one last 'To Hell with the Pope!' before he dies. I remember listening in Court to the examination of an old Orangeman who had been called as a witness to the peaceable disposition of a friend of his. 'What sort of man', asked the counsel, 'would you say Jamie Williamson is?' 'A quiet, decent man.' 'Is he the sort of man that would be likely to be breaking windows?' 'No man less likely.' 'Is he the sort of man that you would expect to find at the head of a mob shouting "To Hell with the Pope"?' Witness, with great emphasis: 'No. Certainly not. Jamie was never any ways a *religious* man.' These bewildering corruptions of sense and sanity overwhelm you at every turn. Ask your neighbour offhand at a dinner in Dublin: 'What is so-and-so, by the way?' He will reply that so-and-so is a doctor, or a government official, or a stockbroker, as it may happen. Ask him the same question at a dinner in Belfast, and he will automatically tell you that so-and-so is a Protestant or a 'Papist'.

The plain truth is that it would be difficult to find anywhere a more shameful exploitation, intellectual and economic, than that which has been practised on the Ulster Orangeman by his feudal masters. Were I to retort the abuse, with which my own creed is daily bespattered, I should describe him further as the only victim of clerical obscurantism to be found in Ireland. Herded behind the unbridged waters of the Boyne, he has been forced to live in a very Tibet of intellectual isolation. Whenever he moved in his thoughts a little towards that Ireland to which, for all his separatism, he so inseparably belongs, the ring of blockhouses, called Orange Lodges, was drawn tighter to strangle his wanderings. Mr Robert Lynd in his *Home Life in Ireland*,[18] a book which ought to have been mentioned earlier in these pages, relates the case of a young man who was refused ordination in the Presbyterian Church because he had permitted himself to doubt whether the Pope was in fact anti-Christ. And he writes with melancholy truth:

> If the Presbyterian clergy had loved Ireland as much as they have hated Rome they could have made Ulster a home of intellectual energy and spiritual buoyancy long ago. They have preferred to keep Ulster dead to fine ideas rather than risk the appearance of a few unsettling ideas among the rest.

It has not been, one likes to think, a death, consummated and final, but rather an interruption of consciousness from which recovery is possible. Drugged with a poisonous essence, distilled from history for him by his exploiters, the Orangeman of the people has lived in a world of phantoms. In politics he has never in his whole career spoken for himself. The Catholic peasant comes to articulate, personal speech in Davitt; the national aristocracy in Parnell. The industrial worker discovers within his own camp a multitude of captains. Even landlordism, although it has produced no leader, has produced many able spokesmen. Every other section in Ireland enriches public life with an interpreter of its mind sprung from its own ranks. Orange Ulster alone has never yet given to its own democracy a democratic leader. This is indeed the cardinal misfortune, as well as the central secret, of Ulster Unionism. The pivot on which it turns resides, not in the farms of Down or the factories of Belfast, but in the Library of the Four Courts. Of the nineteen representatives who speak for it in Parliament no fewer than seven are King's Counsel. In the whole list there is not one delegate of labour, nor one farmer. A party so constituted is bound to produce prodigies of nonsense such as those associated with Sir Edward Carson. The leaders of the orchestra openly despise the instruments on which they play. For followers, reared in the tradition of hysteria depicted above, no raw-head is thought to be too raw, and no bloody-bones too bloody. And so we have King's Counsel, learned in the law, devising Provisional Governments, and Privy Councillors wallowing in imaginative treason. As for the Bishops, they will talk daggers as luridly as the rest, but they will not even threaten to use any. And so does the pagan rage, and the heathen prophesy vain things.

That such a farce-tragedy can find a stage in the twentieth century is pitiable. But it is not a serious political fact. It has the same relation to reality that the cap-hunting exploits of Tartarin of Tarascon had to the Franco-German war. It has been devised merely to make flesh creep in certain tabernacles of fanaticism in the less civilised parts of England and Scotland. So far as action goes it will end in smoke, but not in gunpowder-smoke. There will no doubt be riots in Belfast and Portadown, for which the ultimate responsibility will rest on learned counsel of the King. But there have been riots before, and the cause of Home Rule has survived all the blackguardism and bloodshed. It is lamentable that ministers of the gospel of Christ and leaders of public opinion should so inflame and exploit the superstitions of ignorant men; but not by these methods will justice be intimidated.

And if 'Ulster' does fight after all? In that event we must only remember how sorry George Stephenson was for the cow. The military traditions of the Protestant North are not very alarming. The contribution of the Enniskilleners to the Battle of the Boyne appears to have consisted in running away with great energy and discretion. Nor did they, or their associates, in later years shed any great lustre even on Imperial arms. I have never heard that the Connaught Rangers had many recruits from the Shankhill Road, or the Dublin Fusiliers from Portadown; consequently the present situation disgusts rather than terrifies us. If rifle-levers ever click in rebellion against a Home Rule government, duly established by statute under the authority of the Crown, it will be astonishing to find that every bullet in Ireland is a member of an Orange Lodge. If 'Ulster' repudiates the arbitrament of reason, and the verdict of a free ballot, she simply puts herself outside the law. And she may be quite assured that the law, driven back on its ultimate sanction of force, will very sharply and very amply vindicate itself.

But it is not courteous to the reader to detain him among such unrealities as Sir Edward Carson's Civil War. Treason, that is to say platform treason, is not so much an eccentricity as a habit of Orangeism. It is a way they have in the Lodges, and their past history supplies a corrective to their present outburst. Perhaps their most notable exploit in armed loyalty was their attempt to dethrone, or rather to defeat in succession to the throne, Queen Victoria. This is a chapter in their history with regard to which they are far too modest and reticent.

But the leading case in recent years is of course the attitude of the Lodges towards the Disestablishment of the Irish Episcopal Church in 1869. The records are singularly rich in what I may perhaps call Carsonese. Dukes threatened to 'fight as men alone can fight who have the Bible in one hand and the sword in the other'. Learned counsel of the Queen covenanted to 'seal their protest with their blood in martyrdom and battle'. Ministers of the gospel were all for kicking the Crown into the Boyne, keeping their powder dry, shouldering Minié rifles, and finally joining the lawyers in the red grave of martyrdom.

An Ulster poet (a satirist one fears) wrote a famous invocation to the statue of Mr Walker near Derry, beginning:

> Come down out o' that, Mr Walker,
> There's work to be done by-and-by,
> And this is no time to stand glowerin'
> Betwixt the bog-side and the sky.

But Mr Walker did not come down: he remained on his safe pinnacle of immortality. And of course there was no civil war. That period was wiser than our own in one respect: nobody of any common sense thought of spoiling such exquisite blague by taking it seriously. Its motive was universally understood in Ireland. The orators of the movement never for a moment dreamed of levying war on Mr Gladstone, but they were determined to levy blackmail. They saw that they could bluff English opinion into granting all manner of extravagant compensation for the extinction of their privileges and their ascendancy, if only the Orange drum was beaten loudly enough. It was a case of the more cry the more wool. And in point of fact they succeeded. They obtained financial arrangements of the most generous character, and, thereafter, the battle-flags were furled. Within five years of Disestablishment the Episcopalian Synod was praising it as the happiest event in the life of that Church. The lawyers, being denied the martyrdom of the battlefield, stolidly accepted that of promotion to the judicial bench, and a holy silence descended on the divines.

This strategy having succeeded so admirably in 1868 is repeated in 1912. 'Ulster' has not the least intention of raising war or the sinews of war; her interest is in the sinews of peace. Although she does not hold a winning card in her hand she hopes to scoop the pool by a superb bluff. By menaces of rebellion she expects to be able to insist that under Home Rule she shall continue encased in an impenetrable armour of privileges, preferences, and safeguards. She is all the more likely to succeed because of the tenderness of Nationalist Ireland in her regard. Short of the absolute surrender by the majority of every shred of its rights (which is, of course, what is demanded) there are very few safeguards that we are not prepared to concede to the superstition, the egotism, or even the actual greed of the Orangemen. But it may as well be understood that we are not to be either duped or bullied.

If the policy of Ulster Unionism is unreal there is no word in any language that can describe the phantasmal nature of the grounds on which it professes to fear national freedom. Home Rule, declare the orators, will obviously mean Rome Rule. The *Ne Temere* decree will de-legitimise every Protestant in the country. The Dublin Parliament will tax every 'Ulster' industry out of existence. One is told that not only do many people say, but that some people even believe things of this kind. But then there are people who believe that they are made of Dresden china, and will break if they knock against a chair. These latter are to be found in lunatic asylums. It is indeed particularly worth noting that when a man begins to see in the whole movement of the world a conspiracy to oppress and injure him our first step is to inquire not into his grievance but into his sanity. One finds the same difficulty in discussing Irish politics in terms of the three hallucinations specified that one finds in discussing, say, Rugby football with a Dresden-china fellow-citizen. It is better not to make the attempt, but to substitute a plain statement of obvious facts.

In the first place, even if any policy of oppression were in our minds, it is not in our power. The overlordship of the Imperial Parliament remains in any scheme of Home Rule unimpaired, and any man damnified because of his religion can appeal in last resort to the Imperial Army and Navy. Shankhill Road is mathematically safe. After all there are in England some forty millions of Protestants who, whatever their religious temperature may be, will certainly decline to see Protestantism penalised. The Protestants in Ireland have a million and a quarter, and they make noise enough for twice the number. There are about three and a quarter millions of Irish Catholics. History concedes to Catholic Ireland the cleanest record in respect of religious tolerance to be found anywhere in Europe. We never martyred a saint, and amid all the witch-hunting devilries of Scotland and England we burned only one witch, a namesake of my own. Deny or suppress all this. Imagine into the eyes of every Catholic neighbour the slumbering but unquenched fires of Smithfield. But be good enough to respect mathematics. Do not suggest that the martial qualities induced by the two religions are so dissimilar that two Catholics are capable of imposing Home Rule on twenty-five Protestants.

The suggestion that we shall overtax 'Ulster' is even more captivating. But how are we to do it? Of course we might schedule the sites given up to Protestant church buildings as undeveloped land. Or we might issue income-tax forms with an assessment printed on one side, and the decrees of the Council of Trent on the other. Or we might insist on every orator desirous of uttering that ennobling sentiment, 'To Hell with the Pope!' taking out a licence, and charge him a small fee. Positive treason, such as the proclamation of Provisional Governments, would of course pay a higher rate. All these would be most interesting experiments, and would add a picturesque touch to the conventionality of modern administration. But if we were to overtax sugar or coffee, corn or butter, flax or wool, beer or spirits, land or houses, I fear that we should be beating ourselves rather severely with our own sticks. Our revenge on 'Ulster' would be rather like that of Savage, the poet, who revenged himself on a friend by sleeping out the whole of a

December night on a bridge. The whole suggestion is, of course, futile and fantastic. It is a bubble that has been pricked, and by no one so thoroughly as by Lord Pirrie, the head of Harland and Wolff, that is to say the leader of the industrial North.

The clamour of the exploiters of 'Ulster' is motived on this point by two considerations, the one an illusion, the other a reality. The illusion, or rather the pretence, consists in representing the Unionists as the sole holders of wealth in Ireland. It would be a sufficient refutation of this view to quote those other passages in which the same orators assert with equal eloquence that the Tory policy of land purchase and resolute government from Westminster has brought enormous prosperity to the rest of the country. On *per capita* valuation the highest northern county ranks only twelfth in Ireland. It is the reality, however, that supplies the clue. While the masters of Orangeism do not represent the wealth of Ireland they do certainly represent the largest, or, at least, the most intense concentration of unearned incomes. What they fear is not unjust but democratic taxation. They cling to the Union as a bulwark against the reform movement which in every modern state is resuming for society a small part of certain vast fortunes which in their essence have been socially created. But even on the plane of their own selfishness they are following a foolish line of action. The Union did not save them from the Land Tax Budget, nor, as regards the future, is salvation of the English Tories. Should they ever return to power they will repeat their action respecting the Death Duties. Having in Opposition denounced the land taxes with indecent bitterness they will, when back in office, confirm and extend them. 'Ulster' had far better cast in her lot with Ireland. She will find an Irish Assembly not only strikingly but, one might almost add, sinfully conservative in matters of taxation. As to the conflict between the agrarian and the manufacturing interests, that also exists in every nation on the earth. But neither has any greater temptation to plan the destruction of the other than a merchant has to murder his best customer.

There remains the weltering problem of mixed marriages and the *Ne Temere* decree. It is perhaps worth observing that marriages get mixed in other countries as well as in Ireland. It grieves one that men should differ as to the true religious interpretation of life. But they do in fact differ, and wherever two human beings, holding strongly to different faiths, fall in love there is tragic material. But they do in fact fall in love. The theme recurs, with a thousand reverberations, in the novel literature of England, France, and Germany. The situation occurs also in Ireland. But I am bewildered to know in what way it is an argument for or against Home Rule. Let us appeal once more to colonial experience and practice. There is a Catholic majority in Canada and an overwhelming Catholic majority in Quebec. The policy of the Catholic Church towards mixed marriages is precisely the same there as in Ireland. Does Protestantism demand that the constitutions of the Dominion and the Province respectively shall be withdrawn? Since no such claim is made we must conclude that the outcry on Orange platforms is designed not to enforce a principle but to awaken all the slumbering fires of prejudice. The *Ne Temere* decree introduces no new departure. Now, as always, the Catholic Church requires simply that her members shall consecrate the supreme adventure of life with the Sacrament of their fathers before the altar of their fathers. It is strange that the Orangemen, believing as they do that the Pope is anti-Christ, should be so annoyed at finding that the Pope teaches a doctrine different from theirs on the subject of marriage. The Pope can inflict no spiritual penalties on them since they are outside his flock. He can inflict no civil penalties on anybody. There is undoubtedly in the matter of divorce a sharp conflict between Catholic ideas and the practice and opinion of Protestant countries. That exists, and will continue, under every variation of government. It is an eternal antinomy. But whom does it aggrieve? We Catholics voluntarily abjure the blessings of divorce, but we should never dream of using the civil law to impose our abnegation on those of another belief. If there is any doubt upon that point it can very easily be removed. The civil law of marriage can be conserved under one of the 'safeguards'.

The truth is that in order to test our tolerance Orangeism proposes to us a series of exercises which are a very delirium of intolerance. 'Sever yourselves', it says in effect to us, 'from all allegiance to that Italian Cardinal. Consign him, as Portadown docs, to hell. Bait your bishops. Deride the spiritual authority of your priests. Then shall we know that you are men and masters of your own consciences. Elect a Unionist Council in every county, a Unionist Corporation in Dublin, then shall we know that you are brothers. Disown your dead leaders. Spit on the grave of Emmet. Teach your children that every Fenian was a murderer. Erase from your chronicles the name of Parnell. Then shall we know that you are loyal.'

It has been occasionally urged by writers who prefer phrases to actualities that Home Rule must wait on the conversion of 'Ulster.' Therein the patient must minister to himself. Miracles of that order cannot be accomplished from without. Great is Diana of the Ephesians, and the servitude of tradition is at an end only when the hands that fashioned the idols shatter them on the altars of a new nobleness. Let us distinguish. The Orangeism which is merely an instrument of exploitation and domination will not yield to reason. The Orangeism which is an inherited hysteria will not yield to reason. It Bourbonises too much. It lives in the past, learning nothing and forgetting nothing. Argument runs off it like rain off a duck's back. These two types of thought we must leave to the grace of God, and the education of the accomplished fact. They represent a declining cause, and a decaying party. The Lodges once mustered more than 200,000 members; they have now less than 10,000. There is another kind of Orangeism, that which has begun to think, and the Orangeism that has begun to think is already converted. I said that Protestant 'Ulster' had never given to its own democracy a leader, but to say that is to forget John Mitchel. Master in prose of a passion as intense as Carlyle's and far less cloudy, of an irony not excelled by Swift, Mitchel flung into the tabernacles of his own people during the Great Famine a sentence that meant not peace but a sword. He taught them, as no one since, that Orangeism was merely a weapon of exploitation. While the band played 'The Boyne Water' and the people cheered it, the landlords were picking the pockets of the ecstatic crowd.

'The Pope, we know, is the "man of sin"', wrote Mitchel, 'and the "Antichrist", and also, if you like, the "mystery of iniquity", and all that, but he brings no ejectments in Ireland.'

Mitchel travelled too fast for co-religionists whose shoulders had not yet slipped the burden of old superstitions. The élan of genius and the call of freedom drew him out of the home of his fathers to consort with Papists, rebels, and transported convicts. But his failure was the seed of later success. In a few years the League of North and South was able to unite Protestant and Catholic on the plain economic issue that landlordism must go. That too failed, but the stream of democratic thought had been merely driven underground to reappear further on in the century. In the elections that shook the fortress of Toryism in Ulster in the seventies Catholic priests marched at the head of processions side by side with Grand Masters of Orange Lodges. In the first years of the Land League, Michael Davitt was able to secure the enthusiastic support of purely Orange meetings in Armagh. Still later, Mr T. W. Russell, at the head of a democratic coalition, smashed the old Ascendancy on the question of compulsory purchase, and Mr Lindsay Crawford founded his Independent Order, a portent if not yet a power. So much has been done in the country. But it is in the cities, those workshops of the society of the future, that the change is most marked. The new movement finds an apt epitome in the political career of Mr Joseph Devlin. The workers of Belfast had been accustomed to see labour problems treated by the old type of Unionist member of parliament either with cowardice or with contempt. *Enfin Malesherbes vint*. At last a man rose up out of their own class, although a Catholic and a Nationalist. He spoke with an awakening eloquence, and he made good his words. In every industrial struggle in that sweated city he interposed his strong word to demand justice for the wage-earner. This was a new sort of politics. It bore fruit where Ulster Unionism had been but a barren fig-tree. The democracy of Belfast accepted their leader. They gave him a majority of 16 in West Belfast in 1906 and in four years they had multiplied it by forty. The Boyne was bridged, and everything that has since happened has but added a new stay or girder to the strength of the bridge. And not only labour but capital has passed across that estranging river to firm ground of patriotism and national unity. Lord Pirrie, the head of the greatest manufacturing enterprise in Belfast, is an ardent Home Ruler. Business men, ministers of religion, even lawyers, are thinking out things quietly beneath the surface. The new 'Ulster' is breaking its shell. Parties are forming on the basis of economic realities, not on that of 'religious' phantasms.

As for the old 'Ulster', it remains a problem not for the War Office, but for the Department of Education.

CHAPTER VIII

The Mechanics of Home Rule

The inevitableness of Home Rule resides in the fact that it is, as one might say, a biped among ideas. It marches to triumph on two feet, an Irish and an Imperial foot. If there were in Ireland no demand whatever for self-government it would, nevertheless, be necessary in the interests of the Empire to force it on her. The human, or as some people may prefer to call it, the sociological case for Home Rule, and the historical case for it have already been outlined. We now turn to consideration, of another order, derived from Political Mechanics, or rather bearing on the mere mechanism of politics. Let us approach the problem first from the Imperial side.

On the whole, the most remarkable thing about the British Empire is that there is no British Empire. We are in presence of the familiar distinction between the raw material and the finished article. There are, indeed, on the surface of the globe a number of self-governing colonies, founded and peopled by men of Irish and English blood. In each of these the United Kingdom is represented by a Governor whose whole duty consists in being seen on formal occasions, but never heard in counsel or rebuke. The only other connecting links are those of law and finance. The Privy Council acts as a Court of Appeal in certain causes, and Colonial Governments borrow money in the London market. These communities widely separated in geography and in temperament, have no common fiscal policy, no common foreign policy, no common scheme of defence, no common Council to discuss and decide Imperial affairs. Now this may be a very wise arrangement, but you must not call it an Empire. From the point of view of unity, if from no other, it presents an unfavourable contrast to French Imperialism, under which all the oversea colonies are represented in the Chamber of Deputies in Paris. In the English plan the over-sea colonies are unrelated atoms. You may say that they afford all the materials for a grandiose federation; but if you have flour in one bag, and raisins in another, and candied peel in another, and suet in another you must not call them a Christmas pudding until they have been mixed together and cooked. Those areas of the globe, coloured red on the maps, may have all the resources requisite for a great, self-sufficing, economic unit of a new order. Their peoples may desire that new order. But until it is achieved you must remember that the British Empire belongs to the region of dream and not to that of fact.

For many years now, apostles of reconstruction have been ham-mering out the details of a scheme that shall unify the Empire on some sort of Federal basis. For the new organism which they desire to create they need a brain. Is this to be found in the Westminster Assembly, sometimes loosely styled the 'Imperial Parliament'? As things stand at present such a suggestion is a mere counter-sense. That body has come to such a pass as would seem to indicate the final bankruptcy of the governing genius of England. All the pen-alties of political gluttony have accumulated on it. Parliament, to put the truth a little brutally, has broken down under a long debauch of over-feeding. Every day of every session it bites off far more in the way of bills and estimates than it even pretends to have time to chew. Results follow which it would be indiscreet to express in terms of physiology. Tens of millions are shovelled out of the Treasury by an offhand, undiscussed, perfunctory resolution. The attempt to compress infinite issues in a space too little has altered and, as some critics think, degraded the whole tenor of public life. Parliament is no longer the Grand Inquest of the Nation, at least not in the ancient and proper meaning of the words. The declaration of Edmund Burke to the effect that a member has no right to sacrifice his 'unbiassed opinion, his mature judgment, his enlightened conscience' to any set of men living may be echoed by the judges in our day, but to anyone who knows the House of Commons it is a piece of pure irony. Party discipline cracks every session a more compelling whip; and our shepherded, regimented, and automatised representatives themselves realise that, whatever more desirable status they may have attained, they have certainly lost that of individual freedom. Out of their own ranks a movement has arisen to put an end altogether to Party government. This proposal I myself believe to be futile, but its very futility testifies to the existence of an intolerable situation. All this turns on the inadequacy of the time of the House of Commons to its business. But the distribution of such time as there is, is a revel of ineptitudes. It resembles the drawing of a schoolboy who has not yet learned perspective. A stranger dropping into the Chamber will find it spending two hours in helping to determine whether Russia is to have a Czar, and the next four hours helping to determine whether Rathmines is to have, let us say, a new sewer. The affairs of India, involving the political welfare of three hundred millions of human beings, get one day; Egypt, that test case in international ethics, has to be content with a few scattered hours. And, despite all this, local questions are not considered at sufficient length or with sufficient knowledge. The parish pump is close enough to spoil St Stephen's as an Imperial Council, and yet so far away as to destroy its effectiveness as an organ of local government.

Such an assembly is clearly unfitted to function as the cerebrum of Empire. It must be relieved of burdens which in the complexity of modern politics it is no longer able to bear. How is this to be done? In one way and in one way only, by leaving local business to local bodies. But that is Home Rule, or, as the learned, envisaging the idea from another point of view, sometimes prefer to call it, Devolution. Through the principle of autonomy, incompletely applied, the British Possessions have so far evolved. Through the principle of autonomy, completely applied, and in no other wise, can they evolve into an ordered system worthy of the Imperial name. This is at first blush a singular development. Here lie Ireland and England separated by a mountain of misunderstanding. We Irish Nationalists have for a century been trying to bore a tunnel through from one side. And suddenly we become aware of the tapping of picks not our own, and encounter midway the tunnel which the Party of Imperial Reconstruction have driven through from the other side. Here are all the materials for a *tableau*. Justice falls on the neck of expediency. Imperialism recognises in nationality no rebel but a son of the house. Toryism rubs its eyes, and finds that it is Home Rule.

But, sounded to its depths, this new current of thought appears not only not eccentric but inevitable. Ample explanation is to be found in the history of the Irish fight for self-government. On this subject there has been in Ireland a marked evolution of ideas. O'Connell began by demanding simple Repeal of the Union and the Restoration of Grattan's Parliament. But by 1844 he had advanced towards a Federal programme.

'Beside the local Parliament in Ireland having full and perfect local authority', the writes in that year, 'there should be, for questions of Imperial concern, colonial, military, and naval, and of foreign alliance and policy, a Congressional or Federal Parliament, in which Ireland should have a fair share and proportion of representation and power.'

The proposed change of programme came in a questionable shape to a suspicious time. It was not received with universal favour, and, to avert dissension, it was represented as a mere *ballon d'essai* and was abandoned. O'Connell died, and Repeal and Federation alike were swallowed up in the Great Famine. But time was to renew its urgency. The essential facts, and the logic of the facts, remained unaltered. When Isaac Butt came to formulate his scheme at the Home Rule Conference in 1873 he renewed the Federal proposal in terms almost verbally the same. The Conference resolved:

> That, in claiming these rights and privileges for our country, we adopt the principle of a Federal arrangement, which would secure to the Irish Parliament the right of legislating for and regulating all matters relating to the internal affairs of Ireland, while *leaving to the Imperial Parliament the power of dealing with all questions affecting the Imperial Crown and Government, legislation regarding the colonies and other dependencies of the Crown, the relations of the Empire with Foreign States, and all matters appertaining to the defence and stability of the Empire at large; as well as the power of granting and providing the supplies necessary for Imperial purposes.*

Parnell, who was a supreme master of the art of doing one thing at a time, naturally laid the emphasis on Ireland. But when he was asked by Mr Cecil Rhodes to agree to the retention of Irish representatives at Westminster in the interests of Imperial Federation, he declared himself in very definite terms:

> It does not come so much within my province to express a full opinion upon the larger question of Imperial federation, but I agree with you that the continued Irish representation at Westminster immensely facilitates such a step, while the contrary provision in the Bill of 1886 would have been a bar. Undoubtedly this is a matter which should be dealt with largely in accordance with the opinion of the Colonies themselves, and if they should desire to share in the cost

of Imperial matters, as undoubtedly they now do in the responsibility, and should express a wish for representation at Westminster, I certainly think it should be accorded to them, and that public opinion in these islands would unanimously concur in the necessary constitutional modifications.

That is, if you will, thinking Imperially. Mr Redmond stands where Parnell stood. He claims for the Irish people 'the legislative and executive control of all purely Irish affairs'. But he is altogether friendly to a later and larger application of the principle of autonomy.

But where, asks the triumphant critic not quite ingenuously, is the line to be drawn between local and Imperial affairs? Problems far more perplexed than this have been solved by the wit of man. The line was drawn by O'Connell and Butt, by Parnell and Gladstone. It can be drawn to meet the circumstances of to-day by men of goodwill, after discussion and mutual adjustment. But why not postpone the case of Ireland until a scheme of Home Rule all round either for the United Kingdom or for the whole Empire has been worked out? We answer that Ireland comes first on grounds both of ethics and of expediency. Through all the blackness of dismal years we have laboured to preserve the twin ideas of nationality and autonomy, and the labourer is worthy of his hire. But a Home Rule assembly, functioning in Dublin, may well furnish the germ of a reorganisation of the Empire. If so, let it be remembered that it was not Mr Chamberlain but Daniel O'Connell who first in these countries gave to Imperialism a definite and articulate form. In any event Home Rule is the only remedy for the present congestion of St Stephen's. It is the only tonic that can restore to English public life its old vigour of independence.

Such are the necessities and such is the future of the Empire merely as a problem in what has been called Political Mechanics.

We have now, from the same point of view, to examine very
cursorily the present government of Ireland. The phrasing, let me
interpose, is inaccurate. Ireland, in our day, is not governed; it is
only administered. A modern government, if it wishes to be real,
must above all else explain itself. For such luxuries, so far as
Ireland is concerned, there is no time in the House of Commons.
A modern government must exercise active control over every
department of public business. For such an effort there is, so far as
Ireland is concerned, no energy in the House of Commons. Once
in a blue moon it does of course become necessary to pass an Irish
Bill, a University or a Land Bill. The Party shepherds round up
their flocks, and, for a reluctant day or two, they have to feed
sparely in unaccustomed pastures. Or again, as in 1886, 1893, or
1912, Ireland dominates British politics, and the English members
descend on her with a heavy flop of hatred or sympathy as it may
happen. But at all other times the Union Parliament abdicates, or
at least it 'governs' Ireland as men are said sometimes to drive
motor-cars, in a drowse. Three days – or is it two? – are given to
Irish Estimates, and on each of these occasions the Chamber is as
desolate as a grazing ranch in Meath. Honourable members snatch
at the opportunity of cultivating their souls in the theatres, clubs,
restaurants, and other centres of culture in which London
abounds. The Irish Party is compelled by the elemental necessities
of the situation to speak with one voice on matters regarding
which there would properly be at least two voices in an Irish
Parliament, precisely identical in personnel. Ulster Unionism
presents a similar solidarity.

Whenever a point of any novelty is made, the Chief Secretary's
secretary slips over to one of the Irish Officials who on these occasions lie ambushed at the back of the Speaker's chair, and returns
with all the elation of a honey-laden bee. His little burden of
wisdom is gratefully noted on the margin of the typewritten brief

which has been already prepared in Dublin by the Board under discussion, and, entrenched behind this, the Right Honourable gentleman winds up the debate. Sometimes his solemnity wrings laughter from men, sometimes his flippancy wrings tears from the gods, but it does not in the least matter what he says. The division bells ring; the absentees come trooping in, learn at the door of the lobby, each from his respective Whip, whether his spontaneous, independent judgment has made him a Yes! or a No! and vote accordingly in the light of an unsullied conscience. The Irish officials, with a sigh of relief or a shrug of contempt, collect their hats and umbrellas, and retire to their hotels to erase from their minds by slumber the babblings of a mis-spent evening. And the course of administration in Ireland is as much affected by the whole proceedings as the course of an 80 h.p. Mercédès is affected by a cabman's oath.

So much for exclusively Irish affairs. When Ireland comes into some 'general' scheme of legislation the parody of government becomes if possible more fantastic in character. Let me take just three instances – Old Age Pensions, Insurance, and the Budget. In regard to the first it was perhaps a matter of course that no attempt should be made to allow for the difference in economic levels between Great Britain and Ireland. This is the very principle of Unionism: to apply like methods to things which are unlike. But in the calculation of details an ignorance was exhibited which passed the bounds of decency. Mistakes of five or six per cent are, in these complex affairs, not only to be expected but almost to be desired; they help to depress ministerial cocksureness. But in this case there was an error of 200 per cent, a circumstance which incidentally established in the English mind a pleasing legend of Irish dishonesty. The Insurance Bill was ushered in with greater prudence. The 'government', recognising its own inability to lead opinion, had the grace to refrain from misleading it. No special Irish memorandum was issued, and no attempt was made to adjust the scheme to Irish social and economic conditions. But Budgets afford on the whole the capital instance of what we may call legislation by accident. The Act of Union solemnly prescribes the principles on which these measures are to be framed, and points to the Chancellor of the Exchequer as the trustee of Irish interests. But nobody of this generation ever knew a Chancellor of the Exchequer who had even read the Act of Union; Mr Lloyd George, on his own admission, had certainly not read it in 1909. What has happened is very simple. The fulfilment of treaty obligations required differential taxation, but administrative convenience was best served by a uniform system of taxation. In the struggle between the two, conscience was as usual defeated. The Chancellor, according to the practice which has overridden the Act of Union budgets for Great Britain, drags the schedule of taxes so fixed through Ireland like a net, and counts the take. That, in the process, the pledge of England should be broken, and her honour betrayed, is not regarded by the best authorities as an objection or even as a relevant fact. In the more sacred name of uniformity Ireland is swamped in the Westminster Parliament like a fishing-smack in the wash of a great merchantman.

But let one illusion be buried. If Ireland does not govern herself it is quite certain that the British Parliament does not govern her. Changing the venue of inquiry from London to Dublin we find ourselves still in regions of the fantastic. From the sober and unemotional pages of *Whitaker's Almanack* one learns, to begin with, that 'the government of Ireland is semi-independent.' The separatism of geography has in this case triumphed. The *de facto* rulers of Ireland in ordinary slack times, and in the daily round of business, are the heads of the great Departments. Some of these are not even nominally responsible to Parliament. The Intermediate Board, for instance, has for thirty years controlled secondary education, but it has never explained itself to Parliament and, because of the source from which its funds are derived, it is not open to criticism in Parliament. But none of the heads are really responsible to any authority except their own iron-clad consciences and the officials of the Treasury, with whom, for the sake of appearances, they wage an unreal war. In theory, the Chief Secretary answers to Parliament for the misdeeds of them all. In practice, this fines itself down to reading typewritten sophistications in reply to original questions, and improvising jokes, of a well-recognised pattern, to turn the point of supplementary questions for forty minutes on one day in the week during session. In its own internal economy the government of Ireland is a form of Pantheism, with the Chief Secretary as underlying principle. He is the source of everything, good and evil, light and darkness, benignity and malignity, with the unfortunate result that he is in perpetual contradiction with himself. As we know, the equilibrium of modern governments is maintained by mutual strain between the various ministers. Sometimes, as in the case of Lord Randolph Churchill, a strong personality, moved by a new idea, tears the structure to pieces. But the Chief Secretary knows no such limitations from without. Theoretically, he may be produced to infinity in any direction; he is all in every part. But, as a matter of fact, through the mere necessity of filling so much space his control becomes rarefied to an invisible vapour; he ends by becoming nothing in any part. With its ultimate principle reduced to the status of a *Dieu fainéant* political Pantheism is transformed into political Atheism. Responsible government is perceived not to exist in Ireland. Mr Barry O'Brien in his admirable book, *Dublin Castle and the Irish People*,[19] confesses himself unable to find a better characterisation of the whole system than is contained in a well-known passage from *The Mikado*. I make no apology for conveying it from him.

One cannot help recalling the memory of Pooh-Bah, 'Lord High-Everything-Else' of the Mikado of Japan. Who forgets the memorable scene between him and Ko-Ko, the Lord High Executioner, on an occasion of supreme importance?

Ko-Ko. Pooh-Bah, it seems that the festivities in connection with my approaching marriage must last a week. I should like to do it handsomely, and I want to consult you as to the amount I ought to spend upon them.

Pooh-Bah. Certainly. In which of my capacities? As First Lord of the Treasury, Lord Chamberlain, Attorney-General, Chancellor of the Exchequer, Privy Purse, or Private Secretary?

Ko-Ko. Suppose we say as Private Secretary.

Pooh-Bah. Speaking as your Private Secretary, I should say that as the city will have to pay for it, don't stint yourself; do it well.

Ko-Ko. Exactly – as the city will have to pay for it. That is your advice?

Pooh-Bah. As Private Secretary. Of course you will understand that, as Chancellor of the Exchequer, I am bound to see that due economy is observed.

Ko-Ko. Oh, but you said just now, 'Don't stint yourself; do it well.'
Pooh-Bah. As Private Secretary.

Ko-Ko. And now you say that due economy must be observed.

Pooh-Bah. As Chancellor of the Exchequer.

Ko-Ko. I see. Come over here where the Chancellor can't hear us. (*They cross stage.*) Now, as my Solicitor, how do you advise me to deal with this difficulty?

Pooh-Bah. Oh, as your Solicitor, I should have no hesitation in saying chance it.

Ko-Ko. Thank you (*shaking his head*); I will.

Pooh-Bah. If it were not that, as Lord Chief Justice, I am bound to see that the law isn't violated.

Ko-Ko. I see. Come over here where the Chief Justice can't hear us. (*They cross the stage.*) Now, then, as First Lord of the Treasury?

Pooh-Bah. Of course, as First Lord of the Treasury, I could propose a special vote that would cover all expenses if it were not that, as leader of the Opposition, it would be my duty to resist it, tooth and nail. Or, as Paymaster-General, I could so cook the accounts that, as Lord High Auditor, I should never discover the fraud. But then, as Archbishop of Titipu, it would be my duty to denounce my dishonesty, and give myself into my own custody as Commissioner of Police.

Under such arrangements as these the inevitable happens. The Chief Secretary accepts his rôle. He is, no doubt, consoled to discover that in one sphere, namely in that of patronage, his supremacy is effective. He discovers further that he can hamstring certain obnoxious Acts, as Mr Walter Long hamstrung the Land Act, by the issue of Regulations. The rest of his official career depends on his politics. If a Tory, he learns that the Irish Civil Service is a whispering gallery along which his lightest word is carried to approving ears, and loyally acted upon. Further 'Ulster' expects law and order to be vindicated by the occasional proclamation of Nationalist meetings, and batoning of Nationalist skulls. And he absolutely must say from time to time in public that the Irish Question in essence is not political but economic. This is the whole duty of a Tory Chief Secretary. A Liberal Chief Secretary functions on somewhat different lines. Administration presents itself to him as a colossal heap of recalcitrant, wet sand out of which he has to fashion a statue of fair-play. Having, with great labour, left his personal impress on two or three handfuls, the weary Titan abandons his impossible task. He falls back in good order on the House of Commons, where his party majority enables him to pass an Irish Bill from time to time. His spare time he divides between commending Dublin Castle to the seven devils that made it, and praying for the advent of Home Rule.

In either case the sovereignty of Ireland relapses into the hands of the permanent officials, that camarilla of Olympians. To the official lives of these gentlemen, regarded as works of art, I raise my hat in respectful envy. They have realised the vision of Lucretius. From the secure remoteness of their ivory towers they look down unmoved on the stormy and drifting tides below, and they enjoy the privilege, so rare in Ireland, of knowing the causes of things. To the ordinary man their political origins are shrouded in twilight. They seem to him to have come like water, but unhappily it cannot be said that they go like wind. While they are with us they are absolute, seen by nobody, felt by all the world, the Manchu mandarins of the West. They have been attacked on many foolish counts; let us in justice to them and ourselves be quite clear as to what is wrong with them. Some people say that there are too many Boards, but it is to be remembered that for every new function with which we endow the State it must have a new organ. Others say that they are over-staffed; but all government departments in the world are over-staffed. Still others say that they are stupid and corrupt. As for corruption, it certainly does exist under many discreet veils, but its old glory is fading. Incompetent the great officials never were. A poet tells us that there are only two people in the world who ever understand a man – the woman who loves him, and the enemy who hates him best. In one of these ways, if not in the other, Dublin Castle understands Ireland. Did it not know what the people of Ireland want, it could not so infallibly have maintained its tradition of giving them the opposite. Other critics again find the deadly disease of the Boards to reside in the fact that they are a bureaucracy. This diagnosis comes closer to the truth, but it is not yet the truth. Bureaucracies of trained experts are becoming more and not less necessary. What is really wrong with the Castle is that it is a bureaucracy which has usurped the throne of the nation. 'In England', declared Mr Gladstone, 'when the nation attends, it can prevail.' In Ireland, though it should attend seven days in the week, it could never under present arrangements stamp the image of its will on public policy. The real sin of the Castle regime is that it is a sham, a rococo, a despotism painted to look like representative government. To quote a radiant commonplace, the rich significance of which few of us adequately grasp, it does not rest on the consent of the governed.

'From whatever point of view we envisage the English Government in Ireland', writes Mr Paul-Dubois, 'we are confronted with the same appearance of constitutional forms masking a state of things which is a compound of autocracy, oppression, and corruption.'

Such a system does not possess within itself the seed of continuance. Disraeli announced, somewhat prematurely, the advent of an age in which institutions that could not bear discussion would have to go. Matthew Arnold yearned for a time in which the manifestly absurd would be abandoned. In the flame of either dictum the present 'government' of Ireland shrivels to ashes, and affairs are ripe for the application of both. Here, as in the Colonies, the people must enter into its heritage. The days are for ever dead in which a nation could be ruled in daily disregard of its history, its ideals, its definite programme.

On the minutiae of administration I do not mean to touch. When the whole spirit, atmosphere, and ethos are anti-moral it is idle to chronicle any chance rectitude of detail. If a man is a murderer it is not much to his credit to observe that he has triumphed over the primitive temptation to eat peas with his knife. If a government is based on contempt for public opinion, as its fundamental principle, no useful purpose is served by a record of the occasions on which a policeman has been known to pass a citizen in the street without beating him. But there is one further confirmation of the view, here advanced, to omit which would be to ignore the most significant fact of our time. Certain departments such as the Congested Districts Board and the Department of Agriculture, recent creations, have been freshened by the introduction of a representative, non-official element. Others such as the Estates Commission have been under the control of officials of a new type, able men who do not conceal the fact that they believe in Ireland. All of these new Boards have struck root in the national life to a depth never reached by any of their predecessors. The lesson of this change is the lesson of freedom. In the precise degree in which government trusts the people will the people trust government. It remains to complete the process by a scheme of autonomy that shall make every administrator a trustee and executant of the will of the nation.

There are other organs of 'government' in Ireland of which the reader may reasonably expect to hear something. He will permit me to discharge my obligations by copying out certain paragraphs from an old note-book:

Judges. – It is a mistake to suppose that none of the Irish Judges know any law. Our judiciary includes many masterly lawyers, and many adroit men of the world. But all of them are political appointments. Hence in ordinary cases a man will get clean justice. But the moment politics flutter on the breeze, the masked battery on the Bench is uncurtained to bellow forth anti-Nationalist shrapnel. Irish Judges, in fact, are very like the horse in the schoolboy's essay: 'The horse is a noble and useful quadruped, but, when irritated, he ceases to do so.'

Police. – The Royal Irish Constabulary was formerly an Army of occupation. Now, owing to the all but complete disappearance of crime, it is an Army of no occupation.

Dublin Castle in general. – Must be seen to be disbelieved.

Since there does not exist a British Empire, it is necessary to invent one. Since there does not exist an Irish government, in any modern and intelligible sense of the word, it is necessary to invent one. The common creative mould out of which both must be struck is the principle of Home Rule.

CHAPTER IX

After Home Rule

The advocates of Home Rule are invited to many ordeals by way of verifying their good faith; perhaps the heaviest ordeal is that of prophecy. Very well, people say, what are you going to do with Home Rule when you get it? What will Irish politics be like in, say, 1920? If we show embarrassment or offer conflicting answers, the querist is persuaded that we are, as indeed he thought, vapouring sentimentalists, not at all accustomed to live in a world of clear ideas and unyielding facts. The demand, like many others made upon us, is unreal and unreasonable. What are the English going to do with Home Rule when they get it? What will German or Japanese or American politics be like in 1920? These are all what Matthew Arnold calls 'undiscovered things'. The future resolutely declines to speak out of her turn. She has a trick of keeping her secrets well, better than she keeps her promises. Professor Dicey wrote a Unionist tract, very vehement and thunderous, in which he sought to injure Home Rule by styling it a leap in the dark.[20] But the whole conduct of life, in its gravest and its lightest issues alike, is a perpetual leap in the dark. Every change of public policy is a raid across the frontiers of the unknown; or rather, as I prefer to put it, every fundamental reform is essentially an Act of Faith in to-morrow, and so it is with Home Rule.

But while none of us can prophesy all of us can conjecture, and in this case with a great deal of confidence. On the one hand, Ireland is a country of very definite habits of thought; on the other, her immediate problems are obvious. These two circumstances facilitate the process which the learned describe as an attempt to produce the present curve of evolution into the future. First, then, as to the temper of mind in which an autonomous Ireland will face the world. The one clear certainty is that it will not be rhetorical or Utopian. Of all the libels with which we are pelted the most injurious to our repute is a kindly libel, that which represents us as a nation of orators. To the primitive Tory the Nationalist 'agitator' appears in the guise of a stormy and intractable fiend, with futility in his soul, and a College Green peroration on his lips. The sources of this superstition are easily traced. The English have created the noblest literature in the world, and are candidly ashamed of the fact. In their view anybody who succeeds in words must necessarily fail in business. The Irishman on the contrary luxuriates, like the artist that he is, in that *splendor verborum* celebrated by Dante. If a speech has to be made he thinks that it should be well made, and refuses altogether to accept hums and haws as a token of genius. He expects an orator not merely to expound facts, but to stimulate the vital forces of his audience. These contrary conceptions of the relation of art to life have, throughout the Home Rule campaign, clashed in the English mind much to our disadvantage. And there has been another agent of confusion, more widely human in character. Every idea strongly held and, on the other side, strongly challenged, kindles spontaneously into passion, and every great cause has its poetry as well as its dialetics. Men, forced to concentrate all their thought on one reform, come to see it edged with strange, mystical colours. Let justice only triumph in this one regard, and our keel will grate on the shore of the Fortunate Islands, the Earthly Paradise. All the harshness of life will be dulcified; we shall lie dreaming on golden sands, dipping full goblets out of a sea that has been transmuted into lemonade. This, the Utopian mood of humanity, is inextinguishable, and it has embroidered the Home Rule idea in common with all others. Before the complexity of modern economic organisation was as well understood as is now the case, there is no doubt that certain sections of opinion in Ireland did regard self-government as a sort of Aladdin's Lamp, capable of any miracle. The necessity of pressing all the energy of the nation into one channel had the effect of imposing on political life a simplicity which does not belong to it. But all that is over and past. The Ireland of to-day does not pay herself with words. She is safe from that reaction and disillusionment which some prophets have discerned as the first harvest of Home Rule, because she is already disillusioned. Looking into the future we see no hope for rhetoricians; what we do see is a strong, shrewd, indomitable people, at once clear-sighted and idealistic, going about its business 'in the light of day in the domain of reality'. No signs or wonders blaze out a trail for them. The past sags on their shoulders and in their veins, a grievous burden and a grievous malady. They make mistakes during their apprenticeship to freedom, for, as Flaubert says, men have got to learn everything from eating to dying. But a few years farther on we see the recuperative powers of the nation once more triumphant. The past is at last dead enough to be buried, the virus of oppression has been expelled. The creative impulse in industry, literature, social habit, working in an atmosphere of freedom, has added to the wealth of humanity not only an old nation renascent, but a new and kindlier civilisation. In other words, political autonomy is to us not the epilogue but the prologue to our national drama. It rings the curtain up on that task to which all politics are merely instrumental, namely the vindication of justice and the betterment of human life.

From the first, the economic note will predominate in a Home Rule assembly, not only in the sense in which so much can be said of every country in the world, but in a very special sense. For the past decade Ireland has been thinking in terms of woollens and linens, turnips and fat cattle, eggs and butter, banks and railways. The conviction that the country is under-developed, and in consequence under-populated, has been growing both in area and in depth. With it there has been growing the further conviction that poverty, in the midst of untapped resources, is a national crime. The propagation of these two beliefs by journals of the newer school such as *The Leader*, *Sinn Fein*, and *The Irish Homestead* has leavened the whole mass of Irish life in our time. The Industrial Development Associations, founded on them as basis, have long ago 'bridged the Boyne'. At their annual Conferences Belfast sits side by side with Cork, Derry with Dublin. It is not merely that the manufacturers and traders have joined hands to advance a movement beneficial to themselves; the best thought of every class in the country has given enthusiastic support to the programme on grounds not of personal interest but of national duty. We may therefore take it that the watchword of the Second Empire, *Enrichissez-vous*, will be the watchword of a self-governing Ireland. What Parliament and the State can do to forward that aim will naturally be a subject of controversy. To Free Traders and Tariff Reformers, alike, the power that controls the Customs' tariff of a country controls its economic destiny. Both would seem bound to apply the logic of their respective gospels to Ireland. But as it is not the aim of this book to anticipate the debates of next year, but rather to explain the foundations of the Home Rule idea, we may leave that burning question for the present untouched. Apart from it we can anticipate the trend of policy in Ireland. The first great task of a Home Rule Parliament would be above controversy; it would be neither more nor less than a scientific exploration of the country. No such Economic Survey has ever been made, and the results are lamentable. There has been no mapping out of the soil areas from the point of view of Agricultural Economics, and, for the lack of such impartial information, the fundamental conflict between tillage and grazing goes on in the dark. We know where coal is to be found in Ireland; we do not know with any assurance where it is and where it is not profitably workable. The same is true of granite, marble, and indeed all our mineral resources.

The woollen industry flourishes in one district and fails in another, to all appearance as favourably situated; it seems capable of great expansion and yet it does not expand greatly. What then are the conditions of success? Here is a typical case that calls for scientific analysis. One can pick at random a dozen such instances. Ireland, admirably adapted to the production of meat, does not produce meat, but only the raw material of it, store cattle. Is this state of things immutable? Or is a remedy for it to be found, say, in a redistribution of the incidence of local taxation so as to favour well-used land as against ill-used land? Is the decline in the area under flax to be applauded or deplored? Can Irish-grown wool be improved up to the fineness of the Australian article? And so on, and so on. It is to be noted that of the statistics which we do possess many of the most important are, to say the least, involved in doubt. The Export and Import figures are little better than volunteer estimates; there is no compulsion to accuracy. As to the yield of crops, all that can be said is that our present information is not as bad as it used to be. But above all we have no comprehensive notion of the condition of the people. Whenever there has been an inquiry into wages, cost of living, or any other fundamental fact, Ireland has come in as a mere tail-piece to a British volume. All this we must change. The first business of an Irish Parliament will be to take stock; and this will be effected by the establishment of a Commission of a new kind, representative of science, industry, agriculture, and finance, acceptable and authoritative in the eyes of the whole nation, and charged with the duty of ascertaining the actual state of things in Ireland and the wisest line of economic development. Such an undertaking will amount to a unification of Irish life altogether without precedent. It will draw the great personalities of industry for the first time into the central current of public affairs. It will furnish them with a platform upon which they will have to talk in terms of the plough, the loom, and the ledger, and not in terms of the wolf-dog and the orange-lily, and will render fruitful for the service of the country innumerable talents, now unknown or estranged by political superstitions. It will do all that State action can do to generate a boom in Irish enterprises, and to tempt Irish capital into them in a more abundant stream. And the proceedings and conclusions of such a body, circulated broadcast somewhat after the Washington plan, will provide for all classes in the community a liberal education in Economics. Will 'Ulster' fight against such an attempt to increase its prosperity? Will the shipbuilders, the spinners, and the weavers close down their works in order to patronise Sir Edward Carson's performance on a pop-gun? It is not probable.

Work is the best remedy against such vapours, and an Ireland, occupied in this fashion with wealth-producing labour, will have no time for civil war or 'religious' riots.

As for concrete projects, the Irish Parliament will not be able to begin on a very ambitious scale. But there are two or three matters which it must at once put in hand. There is, for instance, the drainage of the Barrow and the Bann. These two rivers are in a remarkable degree non-political and non-sectarian. Just as the rain falls on the just and the unjust, so do their rain-swollen floods spoil with serene impartiality Nationalist hay and Orange hay, Catholic oats and Presbyterian oats. Will 'Ulster' fight against an effort to check the mischief? Then there is re-afforestation. As the result mainly of the waste of war, Ireland, which ought to be a richly wooded country, is very poor in that regard. In consequence of this, a climate, moister than need be, distributes colds and consumption among the population, without any religious test, and unchecked winds lodge the corn of all denominations. Re-afforestation, as offering a profit certain but a little remote, and promising a climatic advantage diffused over the whole area of the country, is eminently a matter for public enterprise. Are we to be denied the hope that fir, and spruce, and Austrian pine may conceivably be lifted out of the plane of Party politics? Further, to take instances at haphazard, the State, whatever else its economic functions may be, will be one of the largest purchasers of commodities in the country. It is thinkable that the Irish State may give its civil servants Irish-made paper to write on in their offices. It may even so arrange things that when Captain Craig comes to the House of Commons at College Green he shall sit on an Irish-made bench, dine off a cloth of Belfast linen, and be ruthlessly compelled to eat Meath beef, Dublin potatoes, and Tipperary butter. In such horrible manifestations of Home Rule I do not discern the material for a revolution. Again, it may be proposed that in order to develop manufactures, municipalities and county councils may be given power to remit local rates on newly established factories for an initial period of, say, ten years. It may occur to evil-minded people to increase the provision for technical instruction in certain centres for the same end. The Irish State may think it well to maintain agents in London, New York, and some of the continental capitals with a view to widening the external market for Irish products. I do not say that a Home Rule Parliament will do all these things, but they are the sort of thing that it will do. And the mere naked enumeration of them is sufficient to show that such an Assembly will have ample matter of economic development upon which to keep its teeth polished without devouring either priests or Protestants.

There are other urgent questions upon which unanimity exists even at present, for example Poor Law Reform. I have outlined in an earlier chapter the honourable record of Ireland in this regard. We were agreed in 1836 that the workhouse should never have come; we are now agreed that it must go. Whether in Antrim or in Clare, the same vicious system has produced the same vicious results. Uniform experience has issued in unanimous agreement as to the lines upon which reform ought to proceed. At the same time there are differences as to detail, and the task of fusing together various views and hammering out of them a workable Bill will be an ideal task for a representative assembly. But it is difficult to believe that the discussion will be, in all particulars, governed either by the Council of Trent, or by the Westminster Confession

Then there is education. English public men have been brought up to assume that in Ireland education must be a battleground inevitably, and from the first. It would be a mere paradox to say that this question, which sunders parties the world over as with a sword, will leave opinion in Ireland inviolately unanimous. But our march to the field of controversy will be over a non-controversial road. Union policy has left us a rich inheritance of obvious evils. The position of the primary teachers is unsatisfactory, that of the secondary teachers is impossible. When we attempt improvement of both will 'Ulster' fight? And there is something even more human and poignant. The National Schools of this country are in many cases no better than ramshackle barns. Unless the teacher and the manager, out of their own pockets, mend the broken glass, put plaster on the walls, and a fire in the grate, the children have got to shiver and cough for it. Winter in Ireland, like the King in constitutional theory, is above politics. When its frosts get at the noses, and fingers, and sometimes the bare toes, of the children it leaves them neither green nor orange but simply blue. Then again other schools, especially in Belfast, are shamefully over-crowded. Classes are held on the stairs, in the cloak-room, the hall, or the yard. For the more fortunate, class-rooms are provided with an air-space per individual only slightly less than that available in the Black Hole of Calcutta. All over the country, children go to school breakfastless and stupid with hunger, and the local authorities have no power to feed them as in England, and in most European countries. Then again, even where the physical conditions are reasonable, the programme lacks actuality. It is unpractical, out of touch with the facts of life and locality, a veritable castle hung absurdly in the air and not based on any solid foundation. The view still lingers in high places that the business of education is to break the spirit of a people, to put them down and not to lift them up. In token of this, the teachers are denied the civil rights of freemen. Now all these ineptitudes are contrary to the humane tradition of Ireland. Go they must, but, when an Irish Parliament starts to remove them, I cannot imagine Captain Craig, with a Union Jack wrapped around his bosom, straddling like Apollyon across the path. The Captain has far too much sense, and too much feeling in him.

It will be observed that we are getting on. A nation so busy with realities will have no time to waste on civil war. *Inter leges arma silent.* But this is a mere outline sketch of the preliminary task of the initial sessions of an Irish Parliament. Problems with a far heavier fist will thunder at its doors, the problems of labour. The democratic group in Ireland, that group which everywhere holds the commission of the future, has long since declared that, to it, Home Rule would be a barren counter-sense unless it meant the redemption of the back streets. The Titanic conflict between what is called capital and what is called labour, shaking the pillars of our modern Society, has not passed Ireland by like the unregarded wind. We can no longer think of ourselves as insulated from the world, immune from strikes, Socialists, and Syndicalism. The problems of labour have got to be faced. But will they be solved by a grapple between the Orange Lodges and the Ancient Order of Hibernians? It is obvious that under their pressure the old order must change, yielding place to a new. Every Trade Union has already bridged the Boyne. Every strike has already torn the Orange Flag and the Green Flag into two pieces, and stitched them together again after a new and portentous pattern.

What does it all come to? Simply this, that Ireland under Home Rule will be most painfully like every other modern country of western civilisation. Some Unionists think that, if they could only get rid of the Irish Party, all would be for the best in the best of all possible worlds. Why then are they not Home Rulers? For Home Rule will most assuredly get rid of the Irish Party. It will shatter the old political combinations like a waggon-load of dynamite. New groups will crystallise about new principles. The future in Ireland belongs to no old fidelity: it may belong to any new courage.

Assuredly we must not seem to suggest that, in an autonomous Ireland, public life will be all nougat, velvet, and soft music. There will be conflicts, and vehement conflicts, for that is the way of the twentieth century, and they will no doubt centre, for the most part, about taxation and education. But the political forces of the country will have moved into totally new formations. One foresees plainly a vertical section of parties into Agrarian and Urban, a cross section into Labour and Capitalistic. Each of these economic groupings is indefinitely criss-crossed by an indefinite number of antagonisms, spiritual and material. In a situation so complicated it is idle to speculate as to the conditions of the future. A box of bricks so large, and so multi-coloured, may be arranged and re-arranged in an infinity of architectures. The one thing quite certain is that all the arrangements will be new. In taxation, as I have suggested, a highly conservative policy will prevail. In education the secularist pro-gramme, if advanced at all, will be overwhelmed by a junction of Catholic and Protestant. For religion, to the *anima naturaliter*

Christiana, of Ireland is not an argument but an intuition. It seems to us as reasonable to prepare children for their moral life by excluding religion as to prepare them for their physical life by removing the most important lobe of their brains.

The only other prognostication that appears to emerge is the probable predominance in a Home Rule Ireland of the present Ulster Unionist party. That group is likely, for many reasons, to retain its solidarity after ours has been dissipated. Should that prove to be the case, self-government will put the balance of power on almost all great conflicts of opinion into the hands of Sir Edward Carson and his successors. The 'minority', adroitly handled, will exploit the majority almost as effectively after Home Rule as before it. Captain Craig will dictate terms to us not from the last ditch, but from a far more agreeable and powerful position, the Treasury Bench. And we undertake not to grumble, for these are the chances of freedom.

CHAPTER X

An Epilogue on 'Loyalty'

According to precedent, well-established if not wise, no discussion of political Ireland must end without some observations on 'loyalty'. The passion of the English people for assurances on this point is in curious contrast with their own record. It is not rhetoric, but crude history, to say that the title-deeds of English freedom are in great part written in blood, and that the seal which gave validity to all the capital documents was the seal of 'treason'. No other nation in the world has so clearly recognised and so stoutly insisted that, in the ritual game of loyalty, the first move is with governments. With that premised, the difference between the two countries is very simple. England has developed from within the type of government that her people want. She expresses satisfaction with the fact. This is loyalty. Ireland, on the contrary, has had forced on her from without a type of government which her people emphatically do not want. She expresses dissatisfaction with the fact. This is disloyalty. Loyalty, in brief, is the bloom on the face of freedom, just as beauty is the bloom on the face of health.

If we examine the methods by which England attained her very desirable position we are further enlightened. It is a study admirably adapted to inculcate liberty, not at all so well adapted to inculcate 'loyalty'. The whole burden of English history is that, whenever these two principles came in conflict, every man in England worth his salt was disloyal even to the point of war. Whenever the old bottle was recalcitrant to the new wine of freedom it was ignominiously scrapped. A long effort has been made to keep Irish history out of our schools in the interests of 'loyalty'. But it is English history that ought to be kept out, for it is full of stuff much more perilous. You teach Irish children the tale of Runnymede, covering with contempt the king of that day, and heaping praise on the barons who shook their fists under his nose. This is dangerous doctrine. It is doubly dangerous seeing that these children will soon grow up to learn that the Great Charter, which is held to justify all these tumultuous proceedings, has never even to our own day been current law in Ireland. You introduce them to the Wars of the Roses as a model of peaceful, constitutional development; to the slaying of Edward II, Richard II, and I know not how many more as object-lessons in the reverence which angry Englishmen accord to an anointed king when they really dislike him. Later centuries show them one Stuart beheaded outside his own palace, another dethroned and banished in favour of a Dutch prince. Of romantic loyalty to the person of a sovereign they find no trace or hint in the modern period. Lost causes and setting suns, whatever appeal they may have made to Ireland, do but rarely fire with their magical glimmer the raw daylight of the English political mind. As for that more facile, after-dinner attachment, in which it is charged that we do not join with sufficient fervour, it seems to us always fulsome, and often mere hypocrisy. In the development of English ceremonial, 'God Save the King!' gets to the head of the toast-list only when the king has been thoroughly saved from all the perils and temptations incidental to the possession of power. So long as he claims any shred of initiative his English subjects continue in a perpetual chafe and grumble of disloyalty; as soon as the Crown has been rasped and sandpapered down to a decorative zero their loyalty knows no bounds.

The simple and honourable truth is that all through her history England strove after national freedom, and declined to be quiet until she got it. There could not be a better statement of the methods which she employed than Mr Rudyard Kipling's:

> Axe and torch and tumult, steel and gray-goose wing,
> Wrung it, inch and ell, and all, slowly from the King.

It is, of course, a pity that the liberty thus established was better fitted for the home market than for export. But this does not affect the fact that, at the end of the process, the English people were in the saddle. But the Irish people are not in the saddle, they are under it. Indeed, the capital sin of Dublin Castle is that it is a bureaucracy which has seized upon the estate of the people. In Ireland, under its *régime*, the nation has had as much to say to its own public policy as a Durbar-elephant has to say to the future of India. There is just this difference in favour of the elephant: at least he has riot to pay for the embroidered palanquins, and the prodding-poles, of his riders. We are all agreed that loyalty is a duty. It is the duty of every government to be loyal to the welfare, the nobler traditions, the deep-rooted ideals, the habit of thought of its people. It is the duty of every government to be loyal to the idea of duty, and to that austere justice through which the most ancient heavens abide fresh and strong. And until these prime duties have been faithfully performed, no government need expect and none can exact 'loyalty' from its subjects.

But it seems that we are compromised on other grounds. The inscription on the Parnell Memorial is trumpeted about the constituencies with equal energy by opponents wise and otherwise:

No man has a right to fix the boundary to the march of a nation. No man has a right to say to his country, 'Thus far shalt thou go and no farther.' We have never attempted to fix the *ne plus ultra* to the progress of Ireland's nationhood, and we never shall.

What the precise matter of offence may be one finds it difficult to discover. Mr Balfour very properly characterises as the utterance of a statesman, this passage in which Parnell declines to usurp the throne and sceptre of Providence. But Mr Smith complains that it deprives Home Rule of the note of 'finality'. With the suggestion that Home Rule is not at all events the end of the world we are, of course, in warm agreement. But if Mr Smith has entered public affairs in pursuit of static formulæ for dynamic realities, if he wants things fixed and frozen and final, he has come to the wrong world to gratify such desires. And even if he were to go to the next, he would have to be very careful in choosing his destination, for all the theologians tell us that, in Heaven, personalities continue to grow and develop. In fact, if anybody wants 'finality', I am afraid that we can only recommend him to go to Hell. As for the world, in which we live, it is a world of flux. Physicists allow the earth a long road to travel before it tumbles into dissolution, and seers and prophets of various kinds foretell an equally long cycle of development for human nature, as we now know it. The fate of all our present political combinations is doubtful, and no nation has received absolute guarantees for its future. An All-Europe State with its capital at London, a Federation of the World with its capital at Dublin, a Chinese Empire with its capital at Paris – these are all possibilities. Australia may be annexed by Japan, Canada by the United States, or vice versa; South Africa may spread northwards until it absorbs the Continent, or shrink southwards until it expires on the point of the Cape. The Superman may, as I am informed, appear on the stage of history at any moment, and make pie of everything. And not one of these appalling possibilities disturbs Mr Smith in the least. But he is going to vote against justice for

Ireland unless we can promise him that throughout all the æons, as yet unvouchsafed, and to the last syllable of recorded time, her political destiny is going to be in all details regulated by the Home Rule Bill of 1912. This is not an intelligent attitude.

Of course the real innuendo is that we in Ireland are burning to levy war on Great Britain, and would welcome any foreign invasion to that end. On these two points one is happy to be able to give assurances, or rather to state intentions. As for foreign invasion, we have had quite enough of it. It is easier to get invaders in than to get them out again, and we have not spent seven hundred years in recovering Ireland for ourselves in order to make a present of it to the Germans, or the Russians, or the Man in the Moon, or any other foreign power whatever. The present plan of governing Ireland in opposition to the will of her people does indeed inevitably make that country the weak spot in the defences of these islands, for such misgovernment produces discontent, and discontent is the best ally of the invader. Alter that by Home Rule, and your cause instantly becomes ours. Give the Irish nation an Irish State to defend, and the task of an invader becomes very unenviable. As for levying war on Great Britain, we have no inclination in that direction. The best thought in Ireland has always preferred civilisation to war, and we have no wealth to waste on expensive stupidities of any kind. In addition we are handicapped on sea by the smallness of our official navy which, so far as I can gather, consists of the *Granuaile*, a pleasure-boat owned by the Congested Districts Board. In land operations, we are still more seriously hampered by the non-existence of our army. And although, in point of population, our numerical inferiority is so trivial as one to ten, even this slight disproportion may be regarded by an Irish Parliament as a fact not unworthy of consideration.

But we must not suffer ourselves to be detained any longer among these unrealities. A Home Rule government will be loyal to the interests of its people, and actual circumstances demand, for the behoof of Great Britain and Ireland alike, an era of peace with honour, and friendship founded on justice. The magnitude of the commercial relations between the two countries is inadequately appreciated. Not merely is Great Britain our best customer, but we are her best customer. The trade of Great Britain with Ireland is larger than her trade with India, and nearly twice as large as that with Canada or Australia. And while these surprising figures are far from indicating the existence of a sound economic structure in Ireland, none the less, the industrial expansion that will follow Home Rule may be expected to alter the character rather than to diminish the value of the goods interchanged. For if the development of textile, leather, shipbuilding, and other manufactures lessens the British import under these heads into Ireland, it will increase that of coal, iron, steel, and machinery. And Ireland, without trenching on the needs of her home market, is capable of much more intensive exploitation as a food-exporting country. Economically the two nations are joined in relations that ought to be relations of mutual profit, were they not eternally poisoned by political oppression. With this virus removed, the natural balance of the facts of nature will spontaneously establish itself between the two countries.

The true desire of all the loud trumpeters of 'loyalty' is, as it appears to me, of a very different order. What they really ask is that Ireland should begin her career of autonomy with a formal act of self-humiliation. She may enter the Council of Empire provided that she enters on her knees, and leaves her history outside the door as a shameful burden. This is not a demand that can be conceded, or that men make on men. The open secret of Ireland is that Ireland is a nation. In days rougher than ours, when a blind and tyrannous England sought to drown the national faith of Ireland in her own blood as in a sea, there arose among our fathers men who annulled that design. We cannot undertake to cancel the names of these men from our calendar. We are no more ashamed of them than the constitutional England of modern times is ashamed of her Langtons and De Montforts, her Sidneys and Hampdens. Our attitude in their regard goes beyond the reach of prose, and no adequate poetry comes to my mind. The Irish poets have recently been so busy compiling catalogues of crime, profanity, and mania for the Abbey Theatre that they have not had time to attend to politics; and in attempting to suggest the spirit that must inform the settlement between Ireland and England, if out of it is to spring the authentic flower of loyalty, I am reluctantly compelled to fall back on a weaker brother, not of the craft:

> Bond, from the toil of hate we may not cease:
> Free, we are free to be your friend.
> But when you make your banquet, and we come,
> Soldier with equal soldier must we sit,
> Closing a battle, not forgetting it.
> This mate and mother of valiant rebels dead
> Must come with all her history or her head.
> We keep the past for pride.
> Nor war nor peace shall strike our poets dumb:
> No rawest squad of all Death's volunteers,
> No simplest man who died
> To tear your flag down, in the bitter years,
> But shall have praise, and three times thrice again,
> When, at that table, men shall drink with men.

As political poetry, this may be open to amendment; as poetic politics, it is sound, decisive, and answerable.

Notes

1 Stephen Gwynn, *The Case for Home Rule*, with an Introduction by John E. Redmond (Dublin, 1911).

2 T. M. Kettle, *Home Rule Finance: An Experiment in Justice* (Dublin, 1911); Erskine Childers, *The Framework of Home Rule* (London, 1911); Basil Williams (ed.), *Home Rule Problems*, with a preface by Viscount Haldane (London, 1911).

3 A. J. E. Fouillée, *Esquisse psychologique des peuples Européens*, 2nd edn (Paris, 1903).

4 E. G. Boutmy, *The English People: A Study of their Political Philosophy*, trans. E. English (London, 1904).

5 C. R. L. Fletcher, *A School History of England* (Oxford, 1911).

6 Jules Harmand, *Domination et Colonisation* (Paris, 1910).

7 Alice Stopford Green, *The Making of Ireland and its Undoing, 1200–1600* (London, 1980); *Irish Nationality* (London, 1911).

8 L. Paul-Dubois, *Contemporary Ireland*, with an Introduction by T. M. Kettle (London and Dublin 1908) (Translation of *L'Irlande contemporaine et la question Irlandaise* (Paris, 1907)).

9 Edmund Spenser, *A View of the State of Ireland . . . by Edmund Spenser Esq. in the yeare 1596* (Dublin, 1633).

10 Coventry Patmore (1823–96), 'To the body'.

11 W. Sombart, *Socialism and the Social Movement*, trans. M. Epstein from the 6th German edn (London, 1909).

12 Michael O'Riordan, *Catholicity and Progress in Ireland* (London, 1905).

13 Alfred Marshall, *Principles of Economics* (London, 1890), bk IV, ch. 5

14 John D'Alton, *The History of the County of Dublin* (Dublin, 1838).

15 Alice Effie Murray, *A History of the Commercial and Financial Relations between England and Ireland from the Period of the Restoration* (London, 1903).

16 Michael Davitt, *The Fall of Feudalism in Ireland* (London and New York, 1906).

17 E. M. Vogüé, *Les Morts qui parlent* (Paris, 1910).

18 Robert Lynd, *Home Life in Ireland* (London: Mills & Boon, 1909).

19 R. Barry O'Brien, *Dublin Castle and the Irish People* (London, 1909).

20 A. V. Dicey, *England's Case Against Home Rule*, 2nd edn (London, 1886).